DECONSTRUCTING THE KIMBELL
An Essay on Meaning and Architecture

Michael Benedikt

SITES BOOKS

SITES/Lumen Books
446 West 20 Street
New York, NY 10011
(212) 989-7944

SITES/Lumen Books are produced by Lumen, Inc., a tax-exempt, non-profit organization. Lumen, Inc. is supported, in part, with public funds from the New York State Council on the Arts and the National Endowment for the Arts as well as with private contributions.

Printed in the United States of America
ISBN 0-930829-16-6

For my wife,
Amélie Frost Benedikt

Acknowledgments

I should like to thank the following friends, colleagues, and students for their insights and critical readings of the text in its various versions: Richard Brown, James Coote, Larry Doll, David Lever, Robert Mugerauer, Steve Ross, Frederick Turner, and especially Alex Argyros and Kenneth Frampton. In particular, I am indebted to Gong Szeto for his graphic work in creating the diagrams for the book, to Erik Josowitz for his work on the cover, and to Amélie Benedikt for her complete and patient editorial attentions to the language. Ronald Christ and Dennis Dollens of Sites/Lumen Books deserve my thanks, not only for their continuing confidence in my writing and ideas, but for the care they have given to developing the form and detail of the book itself.

Photographs and Illustrations

Michael Benedikt: 8, 13, 23, 24, 59, 62, 73, 74 top and bottom, 80, 81 top and bottom, 84, 86, 89 top, middle, and bottom, 90 top, middle, bottom; Larry Doll: 14; University of Texas, Austin, School of Architecture: 25, 69, 71; GA 12: 31; GA 35: 32 top and bottom; GA 38: 75; Gerald Zugman: 39; Michael Benedikt/Gong Szeto: 54, 56, 61, 64 top, 66, 79, 85, 87, 99, 100; Robert Wharton: 55, 77 top and bottom; E.H. Lockwood: 65; Marshall Meyers: 63.

CONTENTS

A. IN INTRODUCTION

After many years in the air, with the publication in 1988 of Philip Johnson and Mark Wigley's MoMA catalogue *Deconstructivist Architecture,*[1] and the appearance of *Architectural Design Profile 72: Deconstruction in Architecture,*[2] a new "ism" was officially upon the American architectural scene: *Deconstructivism.*[3]

Grumblings from working architects, historians, and teachers of architecture that it would soon pass, that it "doesn't work," that it's crazy, that it's *just* a style, that it really doesn't deserve a name of its own . . . all of these are typical of the kinds of things said at the inception of a new movement.[4] Conversely, the notion that Deconstructivism in architecture is actually all over, come and gone, is also mistaken: Deconstructionist concerns, techniques, and terminology are to be found with ever greater frequency in academic journals of architecture, where they are presented with an ever greater air of normalcy. One must, I think, conclude that Deconstruction is very likely to continue to gain influence in the discipline and the profession, if only as a mode of discourse that supports the real and unstated enterprise of all designerly architects (save for feeding their children): the discovery/invention and execution of new formal systems, i.e., styles.[5]

But Derrida's Deconstruction can mean more to architects (and artists) than a transitory aesthetic or a style, and it should not be allowed to devolve into the esoteric, promotional patter and stylish nihilism that it threatens to do. Deconstruction is primarily a philosophy of writing and reading philosophy. But it is also a probing enquiry into the workings of language, ideas, and the whole human cultural enterprise. As a theory, a philosophy, a method, in the hands of Jacques Derrida and others, Deconstruction had a considerable impact on philosophy and critical and literary theory in the late 1970s and early 80s. As a significant component of post-structuralist thought in the late 1980s, it was still making its way through all the arts and all but the "hardest" of the sciences, representing a pattern of thinking whose generality across the disciplines has been unequalled since systems theory in the mid-60s. Deconstruction's destiny, I believe, like system theory's, is to continue to be absorbed into routine intellectual, critical, and even scientific discourse. Already, key elements of its vocabulary have passed into the realm of common wisdom about method, expression, description, and meaning in all these fields, but its name—Deconstruction—and the name of its "inventor"—Jacques Derrida—may well soon be effaced. Who now speaks of W. Ross Ashby, James Miller, or Ludwig von Bertalanffy?

In the meantime, and perhaps aiding the assimilation of Deconstruction into areas outside of literature and philosophy, we might ask this obvious and introductory question: How exactly is Deconstruc*tivism*—the movement in architecture—related to the Deconstruc*tion* of Jacques Derrida? Do we have to understand the latter to understand the former?

If it is *not* strongly related, we should ask why the new-looking architecture should be called "Deconstructivist." Could it be because of the new opportunities for bafflement that Deconstruction-style arguments give to architectural discourse, or because of some generally anarchic, anti-classical, half-constructed or half-demolished "look" that now seems refreshing? The formal resemblance of much Deconstructivism to the Russian Constructivist movement of the 1920s, of course, has been explicit, clear, and often discussed (hence the prevarication about calling the movement "Deconstruc*tionism*" and being done with it); but why then not "Neo-Constructivism" as Charles Jencks suggested?[6]

On the other hand, if Deconstructivist architecture *is* strongly related to Deconstruction, then we might ask: Just how well does it actually reflect, use, or develop Derrida's philosophy?[7] To hear or read Peter Eisenman is to believe that the connection is intimate and that the result of the marriage something entirely new in architecture. Is it?[8]

In this essay I would like to show the following:
1. that Jacques Derrida's ideas are indeed uniquely significant and productive for architecture, and vice versa,
2. that they most often are not entirely new, insofar as they rename certain procedures and attitudes already in use in modern architectural design and design pedagogy, and
3. that most Deconstructivist architecture—with its angles and "encounters," its shells and shards, disjunctions and "traces," stories and meta-stories—represents only one way of reading Deconstruction. Louis Kahn gives us another.

To show all this convincingly will require expositions of what I believe to be important (for architects) in Deconstruction. I do not undertake to provide the historical background of Deconstruction (and therefore of post-structuralism in general) in literary theory, philosophy, cultural anthropology, and so on. The task is enormous and inherently contentious, and surveys by more intrepid and better-informed writers than myself are now readily found.[9] Nor will I offer any art-historical analyses as to how or why Deconstructivism in architecture "comes out of" Late Modernism or Classical Postmodernism.

Rather, I would look at Derrida as Derrida looks at others: closely, selectively, idiosyncratically, metonymically; centered on works rather than movements, on the telling detail rather than detailed telling. Unlike Derrida's, of course, our discussion is guided by an interest in the phenomena of *architecture* as distinct from those of language and philosophical discourse, and for this reason among many, it will take on its own character.[10]

Further: if my exposition, particularly in the first half of this essay, does not read like those put forward by other writers and architect/writers involved with Deconstruction, then I offer a number of possible reasons. One may be because my reading of Derrida is insufficiently thorough or deep. Derrida is difficult, and I must leave myself open to this possibility. For another, frequently critical of Derrida, I have not hesitated to supply my own ideas and interpretations where they seemed appropriate or to invoke the perspectives of other theorists. But certainly my motivation too is different from many other interpreters of Deconstruction (including, oftentimes, Derrida himself). I do not wish to propound, confound, or promote. Nor do I airily assume the complicity of my readers in the new language game, that round of post-structuralist nomenclatures and odd locutions that all too often substitutes for profundity. I wish only to be intelligible about a philosophy that seems to forbid intelligibility, and in a language, English, which does not lend itself to the homonymic ambiguities of French, or at least, not the same ones.[11] Perhaps most difficult, however, I wish to be intelligible within a cultural milieu that equates the quest for lucidity, depth, or truth with naïveté about the postmodern human condition.

If we can determine that Deconstruction is not entirely new to architectural design thinking (point 2 above), we should not be surprised, or disappointed, or smug. Foregrounding what has been in the background, making explicit what was implicit, isolating what was incorporated, naming what was un-named, and regrouping phenomena by re-view—all these "operations" are central to Derrida's deconstructive method, and all are respectable, difficult projects. Derrida himself does not claim to do anything more than show us how the literary and metaphysical work *works*. His mission is one of exposure: of the tricks, conditions, veilings, costs, assumptions, and procedures long in use in the bending of language to our will, in the transmission of meaning with speaking and writing, and in the creation of *presences*— works of apparent substance and truth—in text. *Our* overall mission might be the same: to expose the tricks, conditions, veilings, costs, assumptions, and procedures long in use in the bending of *architecture* to our will, in the transmission of meaning with designing and building, and in the creation of *presences*—works of apparent substance and truth—in formations of construction.[12] Reading Derrida is an education in how to go about this mission with unprecedented subtlety. Indeed, we may find that the value of Deconstruction for architects lies in the way it can suggest finer strategies for design and critical thought in architecture in general, and not—or, rather, less—in how it might settle questions of the validity of the Deconstructivist label and *modus operandi* for this work or that.

We should also note that Derrida did not build his Deconstruction out of the study of Deconstructionist literature. He deconstructed canonical, classical works: writings by Plato, Rousseau, Kant, Hegel, Heidegger, and others. We should do the same. We should bring Deconstruction to bear *not* on the analysis of a Liebeskind or Tschumi or an Eisenman, who have already "done our work for us," who lie in wait with signed answers to our questions, whose buildings are themselves posed as deconstructing texts. We must apply it to the canonical work of canonical architects—perhaps an Alberti or Palladio, Wright or Le Corbusier—and to everyday, vernacular buildings. Furthermore, whether we select the canonical or the vernacular, we should use examples formally as far removed as possible from the "heterotopic," mock-destructive aesthetic of Frank Gehry, Zaha Hadid, Coop Himmelblau, et al. who are already involved, if with astute distance, in the post-structuralist architectural scene.

Hence my choice in this essay of Louis Kahn, a most serious, religious, and classical modern architect, and hence, also, my choice of his second-to-last built work, the Kimbell Art Museum in Forth Worth, Texas. This highly regarded, serene, canonical, visually consonant and uncomplicated building, completed in 1974, will be the test case for this essay, the focus of our thought. But there is another reason for the choice:

We will not be surprised to find that Louis Kahn and Jacques Derrida occupy totemically opposite positions on the questions of meaning, origin, and expression. How could this be otherwise? Kahn is—was—the quintessential architect and a Philadelphian, Derrida is the quintessential writer/philosopher and a Parisian. One produced a small number of material, ordered, and powerful buildings, devoted to the achievement or evocation of spiritual constants, the other produces volumes of labyrinthine prose undermining every claim to essentiality including its own. Derrida and Kahn are of different generations, did not know each other, and likely did not know *of* each other. And yet we can find them curiously united at the deepest, metaphysical levels, reflecting each other's ideas and media with a symmetry that is as remarkable as it is, on higher, practicing levels, detailed. From studying this symmetry I believe we can come to a better understanding of the situation of both men as thinkers and doers, as well as of the current—and perhaps perennial—situation of their respective disciplines, namely, architecture and philosophy.

And at a more social and perhaps shallower art-critical level: if I can show how deconstructive principles are as fully at work at the Kimbell as in a work such as, say, Peter Eisenman's Biocenter for the University of Frankfurt, we will have to make some choices:

Is the Kimbell a work of Deconstructivist architecture, or not?

If it *is,* what of Eisenman, Gehry, Hadid, Liebeskind, et al.? Does Kahn, with a style and rhetoric and mind-set so clearly different as to be almost opposite to any of theirs, *predate* them? Was Kahn a Deconstructivist—an unsuspected and unsuspecting pioneer? (I am not claiming that very much is at stake here—a label, after all, is just a label, as I suggested earlier. The question is posed intellectually, as a provocation, for what it opens up; and in this sense it is posed seriously.)

Or, on the other hand, will I merely have shown that the

deconstructive project as such is essentially a critical/theoretical one, one properly cast in *language*, like this, and one that is able to uncover and illuminate, through writing and diagrams, certain of the "workings" of *any* significant and reasonably complex building? If this is the case, then we might wonder why Deconstructivist architecture in particular should warrant the (considerable) effort of "close reading" and critical Deconstruction.[13]

Finally, why, if Deconstructivist buildings are wordless acts of architectural Deconstructionist criticism themselves, if they are *texts* before they are buildings, why then are they not best left unbuilt, in the interests of *not* compromising their necessary rhetorical freedom?

This last question is important, and needs to be expanded upon. Mark Wigley tells us that the Deconstructivists' commitment towards physical realization—towards actual *construction*—is real, radical, and unique, inasmuch as avantgarde proposals are usually confessedly rhetorical. Could it be, however, that this "commitment" is itself a rhetorical one, itself a part of the deconstructive critical project? One has only to look at Eisenman's Social Housing on Kochstrasse in Berlin. The deep critiques of architecture, local history, meaning, and method that went into the design of the building verbally and graphically, if they are anywhere on the site, are now hardly to be found. Such critiques are completely submerged within an edifice that has a quite normal share of the problems and rewards of quotidian architecture and one that looks, finally (at the cost of some small interior awkwardnesses), only a little—how should one put it?—"mathematical." Grids at play. So too at La Villette: Bernard Tschumi's follies, if you don't know the critical/theoretical narrative background, are simply nice little red

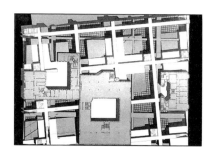

Peter Eisenman, IBA Social Housing, Berlin, 1987.

Neo-Constructivist buildings upon which to climb—which is how the people of Paris see them. On the ground, in reality, the grid on which they are set is invisible, as are most of the overlaid geometrical relationships between elements, and as is the tracing of Tschumi's very advanced, Deconstruction-style ideas.[14] The question is not whether ordinary people can understand sophisticated architecture (they cannot), but whether *anyone* can "read" these buildings *with* the buildings.

No, the critical power of both these projects does not lie in their built actuality. Rather, it lies first in the speaking, writing, and drawing of them, that is to say, in their true and conventional "textuality," and then, at best, in the *relationship* of these texts to the built object. Buildings themselves constitute neither texts nor a true language; their complex of meanings and their subtle powers operate almost exclusively at pre- or non-linguistic levels. This is a claim and a subject to which I will return, for, ironically, it is the very fact that the way architecture means is *not* a strong analog to the way language means that makes architecture the kind of phenomenon which can act as the destination and reward for the Deconstructionist project. It is no accident that Derrida's language—so demanding and perplexing as to offend on the one hand, and so rich in spatial, material, energic and passionate metaphorical motions as continually to seduce on the other—would both point to architecture and attract academically inclined architects:

It is convulsively to tear apart *the negative* side, *that which makes it the reassuring* other surface *of the positive; and it is to* exhibit within *the negative, in an instant that which can no longer be called negative . . . precisely because it has no* reversed underside, *because it can no longer collaborate with the continuous* linking-up *of meaning, concept, time, truth in discourse; because it literally can no longer* labor *and let itself be interrogated as the* "work *of the negative.*[15] *(my emphases)*

Notice the metaphors of motion and geometry, position and withdrawal, construction and destruction in this typical passage from Derrida's prose. Elsewhere, and everywhere, he speaks of grooves, chains, traces, mirrorings, horizons, insides and outsides, centers, openings-up and closings, inhabitations, interweavings, appearances and disappearances. . . . One reads Derrida, and watches a right brain challenging the left at every quarter. Architecture, its infrastructure, its topology, its mechanics, its "moves," are built into Derrida's thought patterns.[16] To deconstruct a text, Derrida demonstrates, is not to read it linearly, or even to criticize what it says by finding objections relative to some other view on the truth claims made. It is to analyze and question a text as one would a site, a building, a marvelous machine, or a set of drawings of these: as something given as a "block," simultaneously, and yet riddled with potential motions, as something whole and patterned yet covering itself up at every experienceable juncture.[17] But let us be careful: Deconstruction is not so much interested in the form per se of language as in the form and motion of the ideational content language delivers, and this is what distinguishes it from pure formalism.

Derrida's struggle, finally, is the struggle to throw away the shackles of language, of "logocentrism." Deconstruction is the invention of a linguistic Houdini. The fullness of Nature—which includes human nature and language—exceeds language's capacity to report on Her: this much Derrida shows us, as others have. Nature's own silence and loquacity exist on other, wordless planes, and this Derrida shows us too—but by default, by "repression" (as he would himself say). Of what? Of arguments toward the realities of nature, biology, and evolution. These are conspicuously absent in Derrida's work—except as metaphors. It is precisely because architecture, like nature, surrounds, supports, and predates language that it permeates Derrida's thinking so thoroughly.[18] But we are getting ahead of ourselves. This last theme will return.

Bernard Tschumi, "Folie," Park de la Villette, Paris, 1987.

B. DERRIDA'S DECONSTRUCTION, THROUGH ARCHITECTURE

To read Derrida is to be swept into an uncanny stream of argument, exposition, and altered terminology that knows no rest or single direction. Language is questioned with language; whole passages swallow themselves up and disappear as meaningful. Homonyms vie with synonyms for possession of the argument . . . and yet "perfectly good sense" is always there, passing below and over, and just out of reach. One learns to swim in this foreign stream, or not.

One claims to have swum, or not.

It is my contention that very, very few people understand Derrida in any detail, certainly far fewer than claim to. In some way this is the fulfillment of Derrida's ambition, the cause and result of his method. Because it simultaneously uproots and affirms conventional rationality in certain imitable ways, and because it partakes quite freely of neologisms, wordplay, and evasions of resolution, the philosophy of Deconstruction is *generative:* of arguments, colloquia, papers, books of critical theory and criticism, and, perhaps, of buildings. But understanding Derrida in the first place—on the belief that he is indeed saying something clear and deep and definable—is generative too. It has created in the last fifteen years a minor industry in academia of lectures, published interviews, explicatory and ancillary books, conferences, debates, and innumerable bouts of academic one-upmanship.[19]

Through all of this one must move carefully, skeptically, and with companions.

Jonathan Culler, in his *On Deconstruction: Theory and Criticism after Structuralism*, educes a number of processes, or principles, from (chiefly) Derrida's writings on Deconstruction that we will find useful.[20] Derrida applies them, of course, to particular texts and (usually by implication) to language as a whole, but he applies them especially to the kinds of texts and the kinds of language that make truth claims and generalizations based on ideas—in other words, to texts of metaphysical ambition. Here we attempt the translation to architecture with a selection of four such essential processes or principles.

The first is the principle of *différance*, the second is the process of *hierarchy reversal,* the third consists in the exchange of *marginality* and *centrality,* the fourth in the relationship of *iterability* to *meaning.* Other, perhaps no less

9

important Derridean concepts, such as the *brisure,* the breach or hinge, *grafts* and grafting, *erasure,* and *dissemination,* and so on, come up in the context of various discussions under the four rubrics. Assuming that the reader will turn to the original material or to Culler and other interpreters for fuller explanations, I will attempt only a short exposition of each—first in principle, then with architectural examples—before looking closely at the Kimbell in the second half of the essay.[21]

1. DIFFÉRANCE

Différance is not a concept or a word, Derrida tells us.[22] Then what is it? Clearly we have just read it on the page, so it must be a word; and it is not a thing or a quality and we are talking about it, so it must be a concept. No explanation will do. We are left with a *koan,* a Zen puzzle, in the position of simply knowing, intuiting, "getting" it, and trusting until then that the puzzle actually has a subject.

As Culler helps describe it, *différance* literally means three things: (1) The universal system of *differences,* spacings, and distinctions between things; attention paid not to a vocabulary itself but the dimensions along which items in a vocabulary separate themselves from each other and give rise to each other; (2) The process of *deferral,* of passing along, giving over, carrying over or postponing; of suspension, protraction, waiving, and so on; a "spacing" in time; and (3), the sense of *differing,* that is, of disagreeing, dissenting, even dissembling. Contracting all these senses of the word *différance* into one is no small task. And yet, if you squint, they can all seem to point in some direction, toward some very subtle and unitary phenomenon. Or perhaps *différance* is a phantom created by the frustration of trying to exceed the boundaries of language in the very act of statement, of positing and delineating categories linguistically nonetheless.

Différance comes very close to the Japanese word *ma,* a word that has had intermittent currency in architecture since the mid-sixties. *Ma* means "interval in space," "interval in time" and "moment/place/occasion" all at once.[23] *Ma* is in the gaps between stepping stones, though we might walk smoothly, in the silence between the notes of a song, though we might sing *legato,* or in the moment a pendulum reaches the top of its arc and stops without stopping. *Ma* is born *of* juxtaposition the way *différance* is said to be conditional to juxtaposition. In this sense they are complements.

Computer science tells us that all information can be coded into a binary sequence of 0's and 1's. *Between* 0 and 1 lies *ma. Because* of *différance* there can be "0" and "1" in the first place.

Différance "exists" as a primary shift, as a first distinction-making. It is the very possibility for that distinction, and the continuance of all systems of distinctions, at once. In the Fall from some unthinkable perfection, which is non-distinction/non-existence, into phenomenal reality, which is distinction/existence, *différance* explodes into infinite real differences, gaps, slippages, reflections and shadows. Feeding the field, the froth, the perpetual play of differentiation, it shows itself as the textured world we witness, the world within which language is but one rather pure—because so subtle, fleet, and immaterial—presentation.[24]

But *différance* can perhaps best be appreciated not from such koan-like explanations as the ones above, but from looking for its signs, or rather, its *traces* in all parties to its operation.

To sense *différance* one must have at least two elements, two members of a system of marks, two ideas in complementarity, or even the same mark or idea displaced from itself into another context. To take an example from philosophy, and from Derrida, one might use that most fundamental and universal of distinctions, the distinction between *presence* and *absence,* and show how, in fact, their difference is their interdependence.

Now, saying that you cannot have the one, presence, without the other, absence, just as one can have no "black" without "white," or no "up" without "down," no "left" without "right" and so on—has been a philosophical commonplace, East and West, for some time. However, philosophy often proceeds as though one could anyway, as though such oppositions were merely philological facts rather than living, phenomenal ones as well.[25] In actual experience, however, the presence of one such phenomenon, say the roughness of an object, has no value, no meaning, and indeed no "roughness," unless, until, and precisely to the extent that its possible smoothness is, at some level, simultaneously contemplated, remembered, or expected. The same is true of presence itself. The mere presence of some thing (even of "presence"), has no value and no meaning, unless, until, and precisely to the extent that its possible absence (and the possibility of "absence" itself), is at some level simultaneously contemplated, or remembered, or expected.[26] Then, unaided, the thing's simple presence stands forward from its possible simple absence. Absence lies behind and mirrors presence always. ("You don't know what you've got till its gone . . . ," says Joni Mitchell. Even thinking of the possibility is sufficient, we might add.)

As a very young man, Jean Paul Sartre recounted, he once did not go to a gathering he was expected at; it had dawned on him forcibly that his *not* being there, his absence, was going to constitute a greater presence than his presence would have constituted had he gone. Hence *Being and Nothingness.* (Later, with much attention focussed upon him, he would not accept the Nobel Prize for literature.)

A couple of architectural examples.

A simple exercise I sometimes give to beginning design students asks them to make two four-inch cubes and two settings, one for each cube. In one ensemble, the cube is to *appear*, to have extra and emphatic presence, to say "CUBE" loud and clear. In the other, the cube is to *disappear,* to have no presence, to be unrecognizable, perhaps, as a "cube" and yet, of course, to be a cube. As one might predict, there are typically many experiments in edge delineation, plane enhancement, and attention-focussing on the one hand, and in blurring, camouflage and distraction on the other. Creativity is in no shortage. One student brought a live chick in a wire cube; another, after placing a plain cardboard cube down on the table, put a hundred dollar bill down next to it! But the lesson learned is always this: the cubes closest to extinction, the ones most minimally indicated or most intensely undermined, questioned, or obliterated, had greatest presence. They held our interest and were really *there*. But the ones most declaratively formed, most sharply set, and materially present were nice but banal by comparison, to the point of effective invisibility: absence. One also learned that this result is not totally wrought by the forms constructed but also by the expectations brought to them in terms of being present or not. Of course. But in this inevitable miscegenation of the two, *différance* has been invoked. Appropriating Derrida's words: "Through a double gesture, a double science, a double writing, [we] . . . put into practice a *reversal* of the classical opposition" of presence and absence, an opposition most "basic" to the multifarious operations of *différance.*[27]

As is well known, one hallmark of Frank Lloyd Wright's style was his dissolution of corners. Placing rooms on a diagonal axis, opening to each other on that diagonal, effectively removed the corners from each room, allowing space to "flow" between them and to improve the feeling of spaciousness. However, the way Wright carried this off, sufficient room/wall was left such that the room-shape of neither was lost. Thus both rooms end up having the "corners" neither really have, with their absent corners mutually "intruding" into each other the way only absent corners can. Their common area is counted twice, once for each room, and from each room.

In the exterior corner *window,* another Wright gesture, a two-fold play on presence/absence is involved. The corner is gone, but not gone (for it remains indicated by sill and eaveline beyond). The *glass* performs its usual trick too: there, and also, not-there![28] Wright's corners and corner windows are elements of architecture *sous rature,* "under erasure," as Derrida names the analogous procedure in writing. A device introduced by Heidegger, with *sous rature,* a word is printed crossed out, with an "x" through it. Thus its legibility, both physically and as a unit of meaning, is questioned even as it is used. One has it "both ways."[29]

We are put in a mind to recall how essential the *presence* of glass has been, in general, to architecture, and especially modern architecture, by its very "absence." One must loosen oneself from art-historical platitudes about modernist glass house, curtain walls, etc., in order to really confront the nature of glass freshly, and in its full meaning. For glass is so

Frank Lloyd Wright, Taliesin West, Scottsdale, Arizona, 1938.

almost-invisible that its presence is always critical. Its acoustic effects, its effects on airflow, and its effects on delimiting the field of human locomotion with the most economical tyranny are profound. Profound too are the multitudinous, tenuous reflections and aberrations that expanses of glass introduce into the visual field, phenomena to which we moderns are sensitized as to few other, equally subtle ones. Architects and students of architecture who treat glass as "nothing," and windows as holes or absences, could not be further from the truth of it.

Mies van der Rohe understood glass perhaps better than any other architect. "The single absolute prerequisite for a new conception of space," he wrote, is that "space defining walls may be reduced to a mere transparent membrane." "[T]he important thing," nonetheless, "is the play of reflections and not the effect of light and shadow as in ordinary buildings."[30] At the Barcelona Pavilion especially, however, he shows us one more binary opposition in the system of absence and presence, one that leads from the nature of glass.

The recently reconstructed Pavilion, with its polished plaster ceiling and chromium columns, its two pools of water, its walls of polished travertine, Tinian and verts marbles and onyx dorée, its tinted glass panels of brown, green, milk, blue, and black, all reflecting or transparent to one another, is a masterful essay in the simultaneous affirmation and denial of substance as *materiality,* and therefore of the categories of presence and absence in general, inasmuch as materiality, at least in architecture, together with light, is prerequisite to presence.

The reversal or inversion of binary oppositions such as presence/absence, Derrida tells us in *Positions,*[31] is only a first and preliminary step in deconstruction, however. The

Ludwig Mies van der Rohe, Barcelona Pavilion, Barcelona,
1929 (reconstructed 1985).

next is to effect, or show, the pair's "dissemination" into areas not, strictly speaking, appropriate. At the Barcelona Pavilion, and then in the countless buildings that have replicated its gestures since, the reflectivity of glass (as in Derrida's *Glas)* reflects onto everything else, as it were. The simultaneous presence/absence of glass is left intact as a characteristic trace, and then multiplied and dispersed out into the whole building, questioning and partially dissolving that which we count on for simple presence and materiality. Columns and walls, with exquisite attention to surface, become mirrors and windows "flawed" by materiality. Hailed (at the time) for its radical asymmetry in plan, the Barcelona Pavilion is filled with fugitive symmetries: the marble veneer grain-patterns are carefully book-matched horizontally and vertically to duplicate the logic of reflection elsewhere in glass, water, and marble, and indeed, any interior photograph of the pavilion may safely be turned upside down and, were it not for the furniture, look unchanged.

There is no presence, there is no absence. There is only the difference between them, always and already in movement, everywhere.

2. HIERARCHY REVERSAL

The preceding discussion of presence and absence grades into this one as we move from binary oppositions into multiplicate schemes of distinctions. First, however, we need to pick up the theme of *presence* once again to show how it is used to favor some terms rather than others in all categorization schemes.

Derrida's "attack" on presence in Western metaphysics is concerted, for he sees two deep problems with it.

First, presence is never simple, the way I described it a few paragraphs ago. Rather, presence is inherently a complex matter. Nothing signified by a signifier is not also a signifier itself, claims Derrida. Because of this, no thing is simply *there,* in, and of, and for, itself either. Rather, it defers its presence endlessly backward and outward into the infinite, self-energizing field of significations, mirrorings, and traces of differences that happen upon each other again and again, as on the surface of some hyperspatial globe.

I differ with Derrida on this first observation, and must expound upon it at modest length if certain later passages of this essay are to be meaningful.

It is my view that although the presence of something *real* is rarely cut-and-dried, the events and ideas that sustain its presence before our eyes and minds as well as in space and time devolve to more and more primal yet fruitfully understandable structures and "forces" (for lack of a better word) prior to which, and below which, finally, "meaning," "signification," and certainly "deconstruction" have no sense. There is thus an *end* to the pursuit of signification. But this "end" is not abrupt. Rather, because it is a matter of history and futurity beyond our ken and of descending *levels* of description, meanings slowly transform away to less complex meanings until there are none that can properly be called meaningful. And this it does long, long before the world is "fully described" by any and all systems of signifiers in our possession.[32]

If there can be no final or originary presence or truth we would recognize (except for this truth that there can be no final or originary presence or truth), then, one should say, so be it! Paradox and all. Less presence, and less truth, is surely enough. In fact, less is *more* in the sense that "meaning" and "truth" and "presence," as well as "experience" itself, are not foundational to, but are the fruits of, evolution. They are its current apex, the crowning arcs of statistical mists gathered and shot through with rhythms unknowable, and whose beginnings and ends slide beyond both comprehension and "comprehension." Presence, like meaning— "presence" of the kind we can think about and therefore that cannot *be* without a thinker—gathers and emerges from *life;* and if we cannot trace it back to some hidden home intact or to the scene of some long-gone gift-giving, if the paths to these last places dis-assemble us as we travel, there is nonetheless satisfaction, sense, and usefulness to *under*standing what we can by setting out to find true origins and ends as though we could.

Derrida's second critique of presence, however, runs on different lines, ones we will find more immediately useful. The idealization of presence in Western metaphysics, he says, causes *all* systems of distinctions and categories to be hierarchical, hierarchical in the sense that one term dominates by overshadowing or occluding the others with its "extra" presence.[33] Even as Derrida points out that *différance* is the source of all categories and oppositions, he also shows us that once a system of terms is set up in some philosophy, the terms are rarely treated as equals. Opposite members (in the case of a binary terms), or absent or "lowly" members (in the case of a list of more than two terms), are subordinated or suppressed, even though they are logically necessary and logically preconditional to the whole scheme. No sooner has a writer or philosopher divided the world in some way than he "valorizes," graces, *distinguishes* one class, one category, one idea with extra presence. *Presence* itself in the scheme presence/absence is a prime example, as is *speech* in speech/writing, and frequently but not always *culture* in the dichotomy culture/nature, and so on.

But the project is futile, Deconstruction shows. The truth, which is that there is no Truth, will out. Close reading of almost any text that makes claims on truth or systematic meaningfulness more often than not reveals the suppressed concepts hard at work, in one sense undermining, but in another sense supporting, the affirmations made on the surface. Paradox is implicit in the language of philosophy, even necessary, says Derrida; and the smooth functioning of assertions, distinctive metaphors and literary effects in a text requires and depends on the submergence, by a kind of force, of the other, now foundational, ends of the paradox. It is as though Newton's third law ("for every action there is an equal and opposite reaction"), had found even more profundity and generality.

Deconstruction thus looks for ways (a) to identify what is being suppressed in some hierarchy or bifurcation of ideas, so that (b) the hierarchy can be undone, overturned, run backwards, or some polarity can be reversed. Why? Beyond reaching a better, if more slippery, "truth," because one finds no loss of meaning in so doing!

One of physicist Niels Bohr's favorite maxims illustrates the point. There are two types of truth, said Bohr: trivial truths whose opposites are plainly absurd, and profound truths which can be recognized by the fact that their opposites are also profound truths.[34]

In fact, one finds more meaning. The thing and its shadow, the mask and its mold, the marionette and its strings, the willow and its reflection superposed upon its roots, the willow and the not-willows around it . . . these *together* reveal a greater meaning, a larger, borderless picture. We see the ideas standing behind the ideas put forward; we see the struggle, the conjuring, the triumph to keep things upright and interesting. We begin to see what was at stake for the author, and we become watchful for how the structures of these oppositions, left intact and problematic, proliferate and reappear in different contexts—in Derridean terms, how they *disseminate.*

For example, deconstructive readings of Romantic works of literature show that the ironic demystification of romantic excesses and delusions that is supposedly distinctive of post-romantic—i.e. today's—literature, was "already to be found in the works of the greatest romantics—particularly Wordsworth and Rousseau—(countercurrents) whose very force leads them to be consistently misread."[35] It is just these countercurrents that gives these works their great, (e)motional beauty. Again, in certain romantic novels, like Nathaniel Hawthorne's *The Scarlet Letter* and George Eliot's *Middlemarch*, although we are led to believe by the lucidity of the language that we are being shown a world truthfully, there are signs, indications, that the author is not to be trusted any more than are certain or all of his characters, who are shown (by whom?) to have reasons to dissimulate. Or we find Thoreau, in *Walden*, spinning a skein of contradictory metaphors constituting metaphysical claims about nature and culture, the finite and the infinite, the literal and the figurative—

each of which is imagined at all times hierarchically, that is . . . one is always thought of as more basic or more important than the other.[36]

Walden Pond reflects the sky, the surface contains the stars, but the stars are also the bottom given way; the Pond is bottomless, yet the bottom is firm and what we seek. . . . And so on. This is not a simple case of mixed metaphors, but rather of one metaphor that ricochets with, and within, its own imagery.

The catch, says Walter Michaels,

is that the hierarchies are always breaking down. Sometimes nature is the ground which authorizes culture, sometimes it is merely another of culture's creations. Sometimes the search for a 'hard bottom' is presented as the central activity of the moral life, sometimes the same search will make only a . . . martyr out of the searcher.[37]

For all this, who would gainsay the beauty and moral authority of *Walden*? Not even Derrida, I would venture. In Thoreau's hands, "contradictions" such as these are like affinitive images, passing easily through each other from different directions. They are figurations and metaphors that are understood together as they move, and that throw us, as they achieve co-incidence, outside the language that has brought us to the juncture. Their fused meaning is singular, and different from the meaning of each taken separately. Deferred, to be sure, and escaping transcription into any other, closed, metaphorical figure that would bring us closer, the singular meaning remains in limbo, intuited, an odor.[38]

But on to architecture.

Because it is so physically tied to gravity, to weather, terrain, movement, labor, and materials, and because it is so committed at the same time to the embodiment of memory, order, and spirit, architecture more than any other art is suspended in a dire balance of opposites: the natural with the artificial, the material with the transcendental, the discovered with the created, the practical with the ideal, the fixed with the free. How does architecture address and then manage such inherent oppositions?

Everything depends on the metaphor by which the oppositional operation is given form in the imagination. Peter Eisenman, for example, has proposed that we understand his recent architecture as an investigation and demonstration of "The Between." A potentially profound idea this, but let us note that the possibility of "betweenness" depends on a certain, and always metaphorical, notion about what "oppo-

Peter Eisenman, Romeo and Juliet Project, 1985.

sites" are. Clearly, with Eisenman, we are to imagine spatially distinct entities positioned such that there can be space *between* them. So we see in his buildings how "betweenness" is overstated, distinguished. Building masses are placed in such a way that each is discrete, and so that the interstitial gap or space between them is maximally uncomfortable, without figural goodness or repose. Hence it becomes more *there*. *Betweenness* as such is valorized.[39] Then too, his emphasis on long corridors slicing obliquely between and through building masses—splitting them apart visually but not functionally, and yet connecting other, distant points functionally *and* visually—also falls into the metaphor.

But other metaphorizations of opposition (and indeed of "the between") are possible. I used one in the last paragraph when I conjured the image of images passing through each other: at the moment they are both there, where is there any "between" in the sense of gap or spacing? Eisenman's earlier work used this metaphor more; that is, the figure of co-planar superposition and coexistence. For example, in his Romeo and Juliet project for the Venice Biennale of 1985 and again in his University of California at Long Beach campus project of 1987, maps of the context—physical, historical, fictional, and factual—are re-scaled and overlaid to give rise to a rich matrix of (mis)alignments from which elements of a new building and a new landscape are discriminated.[40]

And then I spoke of a "*balance*" of opposites. Should we look for instantiations of "fulcra," "leverage," and "weight" in Deconstructivist design? Perhaps. In Zaha Hadid's seminal Hong Kong Peak and later projects, buildings certainly seem to balance on each other like a dowels strung in a mobile, the land rendered as a field of fulcra.

Or are oppositions at odds and "*antagonistic*?" With this as the metaphor we are apt to see forms "attacking" one an-

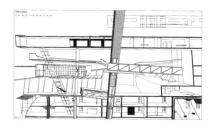

Zaha Hadid, Hong Peak Project, 1985.

other physically, causing "damage": dents, rents, jams, peelings, and interlodgings such as in Frank Gehry's and Eric Moss's work. And so on.[41]

In any field of inquiry it matters a great deal which metaphors are chosen to visualize and sensualize ideas. Though the facts may remain stable, different extrapolations tend to follow from each metaphorical image, and different manipulations seem appropriate (and fun).[42] But it is especially critical which metaphors *architects* use since they are quite liable too literally to build them! Hence the Derridean figures of speech and metaphor that so enliven much Deconstructionist writing—his "forces," "conflicts," and "traces"—in architecture are turned into figures of construction: restless volumes buried like hatchets in each other, surfaces and plans "inscribed" with "traces" in the form of geometric echoes of each other, and so on. Important to note, however, is the almost contentless nature of the action, the vacuity of the "dialogue effected" in the architectural realm. In literary theory, covert contradictions and covert hierarchies are discerned among the themes and ideas and events told of, but the capacity of language to "tell of" in the first place is respected. In Deconstructivist architectural theory, and in Deconstructivist architecture, by contrast, nothing is told of except the process of telling. Daniel Libeskind describes his City Edge project for Berlin thus:

The symbolic breakdown of the wall effected by introducing the . . . motifs of tilted and crossed bars sets up a subversion of the walls that defines the bar itself. Inside the bar

Daniel Libeskind, City Edge Project, Berlin, 1987.

is a jumble of folded planes, crossed forms, counter-reliefs, spinning movements, and contorted shapes. This apparent chaos actually constructs the walls that define the bar; it is the structure. The internal disorder produces the bar even while splitting it, even as gashes open up along its length.[43]

Something rather deep may be going on here, but we cannot say exactly what.[44] Perhaps, like Eisenman's, Libeskind's genius is to have pictured for us, by de-metaphorizing and re-metaphorizing, the very operations of literary Deconstruction in a "building." Derrida himself is excavated, the shape of his inner thoughts laid out on the ground. This is well and good, but the "movements" that Derrida speaks of are not movements in and for themselves, like the contrary and oscillating motions, *espacement*s, and escapements within some watch without hands. Derrida's movements, his "deferrals" and "tearings" and "exhibitings," his wonderful constructions just this side of intelligibility, are detections of the cross-currents and counter-currents of denotated meanings and claims in the text under review. In this sense Deconstruction is extraordinarily objective, and dogged to the point of obsession. As I remarked earlier: Derrida pays attention primarily to the form of the content of the language, and not the form of the form of language.

Now let us look at Libeskind in this project. He can only talk vaguely of "the logic of the city," and of "divisions" as his denotateds, as what he is deconstructing. The "about," the content, is all but missing. There is much chewing but no food.[45]

I bring this critical tone to the discussion because I believe that what the principle of hierarchy reversal teaches us to look for and to achieve in architecture is something much simpler and clearer than Deconstruction's recent exponents would lead us to believe, something long at work in the design of buildings and in architectural pedagogy.

It is not involved in metaphor; or if it is, then minimally. The fact is that buildings can be analyzed along a number of dimensions, into a number of clusters, or systems, of aspects, ideas, parts, categories. These form alternative *taxonomies,* each of which can claim correspondence-truth, elegance, and some completeness in the analysis of what a building *is.* Some of these taxonomies are binary, but most are not. For example, the simplest and most literal (let us think of a house as the subject) might be: foundation system/floor system/wall system/opening system/roof system. A more abstract one: structural system/circulation system/service system/enclosural system/sign system. More abstract still: the order of individual experience/the order of community/the order of culture/the order of nature/the order of physics/the order of Order.[46] There are sub-taxonomies: inside/outside,[47] positive space/negative space/anti-space,[48] and overarching taxonomies, such as the trusty Firmness/Commodity/Delight, or Form/Function. (There are probably as many interpretations of, and variations on, such taxonomies as there are design teachers; and one has to sympathize with the students who must try them on, one after the other, as they go through architecture school!)

All architects, great and not-so-great, face the task of design with some such taxonomy already in mind. The terms are arranged hierarchically. The valorized ones get "expressed," the others "suppressed." Expressed how? By exposure, enlargement, fetishization, special coloration or materiality, and so on. Suppression is carried out conversely: by concealment, diminution, disregard, camouflage. Indeed one can say that *style* in architecture devolves largely upon the selection of certain patterns of valorization and repression, and these applied across one or another taxonomy.

For example, an important aspect of Frank Lloyd Wright's style consisted in the repression of *the wall (*and its "windows"). Imagine a canonical house, a structure not unlike one typically drawn by Western children: a rectangular box, punched with mullion-crossed windows, a well-fitted pitched roof with a smoking chimney, and a path curving past flowers to a prominent front door. Everything important is there, everything is in balance, no part dominates. Now suppress the wall, express the roof; suppress the verti-

Frank Lloyd Wright, Taliesin, Spring Green, WI, 1925.

cal, express the horizontal; enlarge the roof, spread the ground contact, eliminating the "window" and the enclosing wall simultaneously by turning such walls as must remain (for functional reasons) into bulwarks, hearths, or radial half-walls. Those walls that stubbornly still persist, dissolve with shelves and horizontal divisions such as moldings. Fetishize materiality and craft, suppress applied color. . . You have any number of Wright's Usonian houses.

We find Le Corbusier in complete complementarity. He valorizes the wall, and after suppression, transforms all the other elements into something else, usually their ironic opposites. Begin again with our canonical little house. Now, eliminate the roof, making it flat. Here, where we expect non-inhabitation and mere passive protection *from* the sky, create a place of habitation and openness *to* the sky.[49] Question the base or contact-line with the ground. Enlarge it by raising the house on *pilotis* and making a place of life and space and motion out of what was previously merely a squeezed zone of shrubbery, a muddy line. Now the wall. Free it everywhere from structural duty by dodging columns and by cutting it open with large horizontal windows that are not windows but strips of absence, yet insist on the wall's presence as a wall and on the house as a box of such walls. Disregard materiality and craft, emphasize applied color. . . You have the style, but not the substance of course, of Villa Savoye.

Robert Venturi valorized the window, insisted on it. Oversize, square (usually slightly horizontal, just to make it "worse"), be-mullioned into four, and oddly placed on half levels and too near corners, Venturi challenged the Modernist denial of the window as a window by reinstating it with a vengeance, and suppressing in turn elements dear to Modernists such as structure, openness, and services. So too his treatment of walls with decorative patterning, possibili-

Le Corbusier, Villa Savoye, 1931.

ties repressed by Modernism's attention to pure geometry and spatiality.

One of Louis Kahn's discovered and quite new taxonomies was his now well-known division of buildings into "served" and "servant" spaces. Relative to the norm, he valorized servant spaces.

How far back in history can one go with this play? The difficult columnar architecture chosen for the sacred buildings of ancient Egypt and Greece can be seen as the repression, or rejection in kind, of the easy, "mural," cellular architecture of the everyday city. In the canonical case, the Greek temple stands alone on a hill, the *cella* retreats and is colored dark, leaving the columns to stand aligned in the sunshine, on a podium, holding the roof and the roof only, as bearers might carry a litter or coffin. The podium is just so high that its top aligns with the eye level of a viewer nearby, and coincides with the Aegean horizon. In this way the column is always seen against the sky, as though springing directly from the earth. Fluted, curved, spaced just so, the column is now further valorized; as indeed later it is fetishized by the Romans who placed it on pedestals, elaborated it, slenderized it, decontextualized it, and framed and presented it in every way as: A Column.[50]

In sum, *this* architecture champions structure, *that* one surface; *this* one champions canonical forms, *that* one deviations from canonical forms. *This* architecture is "socially responsible," *that* one is "mere formalism." And so forth. But each architecture that valorizes any element of a taxonomy suppresses the others upon which the valorization depends,

Robert Venturi, Brant Ski House, Colorado, 1971.

and thus, somewhat ironically, calls attention to them. How? If not simply by their conspicuous absence, as we say, then by signs of the scuffle.[51]

This kind of analysis may seem a little cold-blooded—as though the evolution of architectural styles were nothing more than the periodic play in the hierarchical ordering of the elements of certain rather boring-in-themselves tax-onomies of the phenomenon of architecture. The analysis seems to diminish the import of historical context and of the grand architectural philosophies, visions, principles, and ar-guments that have guided the evolution of the discipline. It seems to make of them all mere rationalizations masking a shallow appetite for distinction and novelty for their own sakes. But it does not, and should not, for a number of rea-sons.

Firstly, these "morphological games" are awfully difficult to play and win, if by winning one means establishing a new canon more suited to the temper and technology of the age. But secondly, and more importantly, the analysis suggests that the deeper art of architecture lies not in the surprising variation of play in the game of expression/repression with-in a given taxonomical scheme, but in the invention of new taxonomies, or the revision and enlargement of old ones as well. For it is from among the key terms of a new or revised taxonomy that a new music of differences can arise.

Kahn's "served" and "servant" spaces was such a inven-tion. (He made others.) Universal, redirecting, opening up new opportunities for valorizations and repressions, this brilliant but simple taxonomy well suited an age of super-plumbing, electrical wiring, communications, air condition-ing, fire escapes, elevators, highways, and parking garages. It influenced the work of a generation of architects, from Paul Rudolph to Richard Rogers, and continues to do so in smaller ways today in every building that exposes, collects, or gives good room and good form to its "services."

Le Corbusier's incisions into the corpus of the canonical building—between floor and earth with *pilotis*, between window and air with *bris soleil*, between roof and sky with roof gardens—were not only reversals in hierarchy, but un-burials, inventions that expanded old taxonomies of build-ing-parts quite literally by opening up—wedging apart—what was closed, and by positing light, large, and functional entities in the dark of unnoticed betweens. Parallel to this, his later use of *beton brut* allowed him to accomplish an essentially deconstructive double move: *having* intense materiality, while not having to *care* about materiality. With this split of materiality from craft he showed the way to a natural artificiality, an artificial naturalism. No Ruskinian entranced by craft and first-order intentionality could have envisaged this.

In all, it is hard to overemphasize just how prevalent taxonomic hierarchies are in architecture, and not just the obvious formal ones. This is why architecture is so prone to Deconstruction, and why Deconstruction is so prone, as it were, to architecture.

One has only to think of the suppressions, valorizations, and concealments involved in that most common pair of architectural productions by which we "know" interesting buildings: the magazine photograph and its accompanying text. Set aside the text. Many famous buildings may neither be visited at any time nor fully—that is, front and back, inside and out. Much is "off limits." There are official views (in both senses of the word "views") that forbid pictures of what would undermine, belie, or embarrass. Privacy is as often as not a pretext.

Then too, many architects design with a single *mise en scène* in mind anyway, and from the outset: they contrive only the picture, the spectacle, that will be published and/or by which the building will be known to most. This single scene subjugates all other aspects of the design and the claims these other aspects have to the resources of the project. Indeed, this is the essence of the scenographic mode of design. Is there nothing else worth seeing (for a visitor) in the building? Perhaps we are to suppose that the single spectacle we *can* witness is repeated elsewhere, in places we cannot reach. Then the one *mise en scène* to which we have been permitted access—this one—is merely an *example* of those others which, by their very inaccessibility and privacy, themselves become more meaningful. Now, yet greater value is conferred upon the present, lucky prospect! The ramifications go on.

All this is on top of the fact that, by nature, a building conceals much of what makes it up: from its structure and inner materials, through its service areas and functionally private spaces, to the budgets, the programs, the disputes and resolutions, that went into giving it shape.

The close reading Deconstructionist analysis requires of

texts such as books is therefore very difficult to achieve in architecture. Books are completely accessible physically. They are portable, possessible, mark-able and re-viewable. Buildings only rarely can be any of these for their "readers." True, the novel hides from us much of what "really" is in the author's mind, as may the metaphysical text, and, true, both may use certain omissions for effect, but neither conceals what is essential for experiencing the text itself wholly (let alone what is essential for understanding it) quite so determinedly as does a notable building. As a result, more often than not, the "better known" a building is the less known it is. The student of architecture is dependent on one or two texts-become-standard, and a handful of pictures. Maison de Verre, by Pierre Chareau and Bernard Blijvoet, is a prime example. The perceptual/intellectual effort called for in an analysis by Deconstruction of a good building may begin to match the effort of the building's designer, just as it may the original writer's in literary criticism. Intimacy with the work is crucial, and Deconstruction as a critical enterprise in architecture cannot be done, or done well, "on the fly," from a few photographs or visits, which is the way almost all architectural criticism and theorizing from buildings is accomplished.[52]

3. MARGINALITY AND CENTRALITY

Having laid out two major aspects of Deconstruction, we are able to move more quickly. Derrida's ideas are richly interconnected and mutually dependent, as one might expect. Most seem to issue from the (non!)concept of *différance*, and overlap each other in proliferating near-synonymity. "Marginality" and "centrality," the case in point, for example, can be used in the sense of "not-important" and "important" respectively, and thus blend quite well into the argument we have just completed about hierarchies, valorizations, and their "reversals." The way to avoid repetition in the argument here is to take more literally the *spatiality* of the metaphor enunciated by the marginal-central opposition. Then, when we reverse or balance out the *importance* of each (which, by now, the reader will expect Derrida to insist that we do!), and look for their recurrence in dissemination, we will be able to do so independently of their spatial character. We will be able to hold on to a picture of centers and margins still operating in their place, as it were, but in opposition to their natural meaning.

Margins imply closeness to limits, outside edges, and boundaries along which what is "inside" becomes "outside." The word "margin" has directionality built into its meaning: the direction to the center or central region. Margins are close to thresholds (which have the related directionality of crossing), but are themselves not the thresholds. Margins have an area, and adjoin and include the inside border of the border.

Centers, in complement, imply the notions of depth and heart, the place of concentrated meaning and "gravity," the points at which action originates from within and the destination at which it finally arrives from without. Centers are also defined by their embeddedness, their insideness, or their remoteness from the outside in every direction. If outside there is danger, then in the marginal zone there is precaution, and at the center, security.

With these two short paragraphs, I have done little but provide one field of meanings for the concepts of centrality and marginality to operate in. I have omitted the political dimension of the opposition—that is, where the avant-garde, the insane, the disenfranchised and the dispossessed are said to be at the margins of society, and those who are established, sane, in power, and "where it's at," are said to be at the center. Derrida and others make good use of this interpretation.[53] I will not, however; even though there is much that could be said about the newly-noted architect's typically ambivalent relationship to his or her vanishing marginality. Nor will I discuss the critical, art-historical practice of discovering, reevaluating, and rehabilitating little-known, or marginal, artists and architects (and/or little-known works and parts of works by the renowned) in a bid to invert the current central-marginal judgment of the artist and his work, and, perhaps not incidentally, of the critic and his. Rather, I would look at the simplest and least metaphorical instances, those in the building itself: *its* margins, *its* centers, at what happens at the periphery and at the heart spatially.

Immediately one runs into a problem: the problem of banality. For the discussion of such fundamental ideas is apt, on the one hand, to run on and on, citing building after building in the manner of a design class on the "elements of architecture," or, on the other, to be cursory and trivial even if deadly true. After all, what building cannot be said to have a center or centers and margins of some sort as a simple fact of geometry? Only when we see central and marginal "moves" exchanged or challenged or repressed deconstructively are they interesting; only then do we seem to see them at all.

So let me make some not entirely cursory remarks about the canonical, or "correct," treatment of margins and centers in a building, the ones we will soon find deconstructed at the Kimbell.

The peripheral zone of a room, near the wall, is always set aside for a consistent use; in the West for furniture, in the East (Japan) for circulation around furniture. In both cases, the center of the room is the place for speech and decision, the margin the place for whispers and commentary; the center is the stage for action and performance, the margin is set aside for serving and witnessing.

When this peripheral zone is doubly marginal, that is, when the zone belongs not only to the periphery of a room as a room among rooms, but to the periphery of the building as a whole, as happens alongside walls to the outside, this setting-aside is stronger. Here we find: windows, doors, and shutters, and provision for the swing of their leaves; preparations for egress and postludes to ingress such as mats and coat-racks and small tables; heaters, sills, seats, hooks, layers of curtains, pelmets, and all manner of items such as chairs, music stands, and tables dedicated to benefitting from the air, or light, or view afforded by closeness to the threshold to outdoors. In layout, this is not unlike the margins on a page of text. This marginal area has a breadth, a thickness, often involving the thickness of the wall as such, where light is reflected and softened by floors, sills, soffits, and reveals. The "bay window" is precisely an invention that enlarges this marginal zone, making it that much more inhabitable. But it starts a movement that must stop before the space reaches the status of a room in its own right, with its own margins.

Now, architecture that uses thick (especially exterior) walls has a natural advantage in establishing and complementing marginal zones. Since this includes most pre-modern architecture, it is interesting to see how certain modernists attempted to retain the spatial margin with their thin-walled systems, and how others, usually to the detriment of the building and its use, let it disappear.

The exterior walls at Villa Savoye, for example, are perhaps ten centimeters thick, which is to say, thin. Therefore Le Corbusier does everything he can to move "things" to the wall, especially in the neighborhood of windows: shelves, seats, heaters, articulations in the ceiling. Structural columns are pulled back to stand alone, not at just any distance from the exterior walls, but around eighty centimeters, and aligned so as to create a demarcated layer of space that is not useless, but is not usable in the same way the center of the room is.

Similarly, Frank Lloyd Wright brings habitability to the exterior wall (and indeed all margins) with window seats, cabinets, ceiling drops, and a variety of "built-in" furniture that draws habitation toward and into the (not)wall.

Only in the work and legacy of Mies van der Rohe does one see, as a rule, an ignoring or repressing of the issue of margins. The glass curtain wall, to be a "curtain," must avoid contamination by the abutment of things. From around the free-standing furniture, one walks to the "wall" and stares out or down, the margin condensed tautly to a matter of inches, indeed, dissipating instantly to the outdoors. As for interior margins, something equally minimal applies: all the work of "margination" is done by the relationship of the carpet to the larger room. One is on or off the carpet, in or out of the furniture grouping. The uncarpeted floor is thus the margin; and the success of the whole mechanism depends on there being enough space—sufficient area—for furniture groupings to complete themselves one margin's-width away from the borders.

This kind of minimalism is not the same as repression, or need not be. As in the case of the basic design exercise with cubes I described earlier, the very tenuousness of a form can

Philip Johnson, Johnson House, Connecticut, 1949.

vivify it. But the danger of extinction exists always, Derrida notwithstanding, and one must take note of the vast number of thin-walled buildings today—houses, apartment buildings, offices—that provide windows and doors simply as incidents of puncture, without preparation, without aftermath, without margination of any kind. Often, rooms are too small to use floor space itself (relative to furniture groupings) to create margins, and fixtures such as shelves and cabinets are so "built in" and flush as to lose any marginating power they might have.

Centers and centrality offer another rich field of converse instantiations and demonstrations. Usually protected by physical, social, and psychological thresholds, centers exist somewhere within buildings (and cities) as places of arrival and rest, as loci of decision and performance, and often as sources of energy and strength, quite literally.[54] At the center we find confluences of axes, motions and indications.

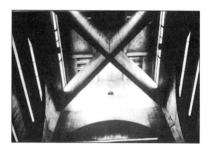

Louis Kahn, Exeter Library, New Hampshire, 1972.

Louis Kahn, Exeter Library

There is often a compaction of information and meaning, accompanied by a paradoxical release into other and other-worldly spaces, as though the relationship of center to margin has been turned inside out. And so on.[55]

Important to note is the interdependence of center and margin, the incredible *givenness* of the difference in geometrical reality, and the power that flows from challenging, without destroying, the pattern. At the Exeter Library, Louis Kahn shows a way, as we will see him do again more masterfully at the Kimbell:

It is common in the design of libraries to place the books in the center and the reading areas around the perimeter. This "says" that the existence, if not the content, of books is central, while the fact that you read them is peripheral. In other designs, the librarians' control desk is central, the book stacks peripheral, and the reading of takes place in between. This is a common pattern at American suburban branch libraries, and the meaning is easy to figure out. In Labrouste's Bibliothèque Nationale and Bibliothèque Genèvieve, as in many traditional libraries the world over built at a time when the book was valorized, the margins of a tall central space are book-lined, with catwalks and ladders for access where needed. The center is occupied by readers at tables. Under individual lamps, bending into books, surrounded by books, readers thus become centers within the center, page by page, opening spaces within space.

At Exeter, Louis Kahn does the following: he situates reading stations around the periphery, attracted by the light. But each station is so centered unto itself and so particularized in utility and craft as to undo the marginalization implied. The ceiling around this space is, accordingly, surprisingly high, valorizing the act of reading. At the geometrical center of the building, there is nothing but a void, a tall emptiness lit from above with circles inscribed toward it as though to describe, to trace, an invisible, unstatable something-unitary hovering in the middle. Thus the center is both empty and full. The book stacks lie between this center and the periphery, aligned between the ineffable light and the everyday light, the ideal and the circumstantial, the one and the many, as though the medium for transitions, while the books themselves crowd in rows and darkness, like unopened pages. The librarians are nowhere special but in the right place functionally, and thus invisible.

I do not wish to enter the debate too deeply here as to the status of *ornamentation* and *detail.* The topic is enormous. But, clearly, the theme of marginality versus centrality is present not just in the sense of unimportant/important, but in relation to the fact that much architectural ornamentation is quite literally to be found on and around the sides, edges, boundaries, joints, and transition areas between functional elements.[56] These are marginal physically, and, as we all know, as though to compound the metaphor, Modernist dogma after Adolf Loos had it that ornamentation was superfluous, decadent, and was to be banished if essentiality and honesty, i.e., the *presence* of true architecture, was to be achieved. Notice that Loos called ornament a *crime.* The intensity of the scorn he directed at the marginal and unnecessary gives us reason to believe that ornamentation was not marginal at all, at least not to Loos. To the truly marginal we feel indifference, not anger. Did he, and the Modernists, not depend on the existence of ornamentation as context in order to energize the dialectic? Do we not see in many of Loos's buildings ornament creeping back, abashed, and rather lovely? And in the love of Modernist architects for the intricate detail, albeit technological and small scale, do we not see the longing for ornament sublimated? One thinks here of the work of Carlo Scarpa, and his care specifically for edges and thresholds, almost obsessively multiply inscribed and stated.

Derrida, in *The Truth in Painting,* speaks of the *parergon* (*para* = beside, *ergon* = work), that is, the *frame* of a painting as essential in not only negotiating the distinction between wall and work-of-art, providing there the primary sign of valorization by which the art becomes Art—that purveyor of Truth excised from and incised into Life—but also of how the frame contains within its own logic, its own zone of expertise and discourse, a parallel commentary and "essential supplement" to the work, the *ergon.* Likewise: the pedestal, the plinth, the podium, the surround, we might say, negotiates the distinction between the sculpture, or building, as "figure" and nature as "ground," and so on. Why, if they were not important, do such margins receive so much craft and decorative attention across almost all cultures and all times? The logic of the *parergon* can be carried on ad infinitum. How can we say, except by fiat or exasperation, *what* is ultimately presented in and for itself? What is it that is without need of framing; and yet what framing cannot be seen as embellishment? Derrida seems to ask the question in a new way.[57]

One more meditation on the issue of marginality, centrality, and the *parergon*: The foreword, the frontispiece, introduction, the preface, the footnote,[58] the parenthesis, the aside, the quotation mark, the afterword, the appendix, the supplement, the commentary, the cover note, the review . . . all these and all the smaller paraphernalia of textuality are, for Derrida, parergonal too, ready for a Deconstructionist role reversal with what is central. For sometimes, like an exoskeleton, they support the softer interior entirely, and are therefore functionally central. Sometimes they are like pockets, storing essential nutrients, and sometimes they perform a vignetting function—an area for rapid strokes that blend and fade the edges of the text into the ground of belonging, dissimulating differences. It is often here, in the marginalia of the text proper, that the repressed yet essential concepts of the text find a home, and it is often from here that a deconstructive critical appraisal can be staged.

In architecture, there are constructions parallel to the textual ones mentioned. I think they can be divided again into two classes.

First: those parts of a building (and its site) that are "extras," such as porches, plazas, planting, greenhouses, machine rooms, servant's quarters, shutters, garages, storerooms, antennae, sculptures, garden furniture, driveways, and so forth. It is easy to show that, for most people, these extras are essential and telling, and that what architects regard as central—such as proportionality, meaning, structural integrity, honesty of materials, and the rest—are, for most people, marginal and mute. (A Deconstructivist architecture that looks almost solely to such "marginalia" for emphasis would be quite original today, and quite different from the Deconstructivist style put forward so far.)

The second class of physically and critically marginal constructions that we can identify are the extensions, additions, alterations, and renovations common to architectural practice. These all stand outside, alongside, or inside the original "text," qualifying it in some way, challenging it in some way, if only with their newness. When additions are made to canonical works dissention is the rule; witness the uproar over Michael Graves's recent proposal for expanding the Whitney Museum by Marcel Breuer, the contention over Gwathmey/Siegel's proposal to add to the Guggenheim Museum by Frank Lloyd Wright, or the fate of Romaldo Giurgola's proposal for additions to the Kimbell (which we will have reason to discuss in detail later). Why? Only because the architectural addition must, in defining itself, define also the work being added to. Consider the rhetorical positions that the addition can adopt. Does the addition function as a *supplement,* that is, as something that would complete what was incomplete? If so, what does it mean to complete what the original architect thought *was* complete? How originary was his "original" anyway? Is the addition a replication, or an outgrowth, of the original? Or is it a challenge, an infiltration, a recasting of the very taxonomy that undergirds the articulations of the original? The designer must decide which image of the situation he will proceed with. Each carries its own force.

Indeed, one might say that it is with additions and remodelings that Deconstruction, as a set of meaningful ideas and design strategies, has its most "natural home" in architecture. This would be quite in accordance with the thrust of Derrida's Deconstruction, which is a mode of criticism first and of *ab initio* philosophizing second, and whose efforts are often so undividedly focussed on a prior text of equal or greater magnitude to the one being produced. If I am correct, then Frank Gehry's ongoing operations on his house in Santa Monica ought to be the paradigmatic example of the Deconstructivist project.

Finally, pure *renovation* projects in particular are interesting, since they reduce the architect's intervention to a kind of minimum, and yet release no less power in the realm of real social meaning. In the practice of renovation and restoration almost nothing is done but to take the processes of renewal and copying-over to some satisfactory conclusion. And yet here, once the building has been assigned value enough to be preserved or renovated, *fidelity* to the original becomes the unspoken value, and opportunities for deconstruction arise en masse. Contradictions are hatched from the very premise of the project. What was the old building "like"? Why fix it? On what criteria has one succeeded? One is thrown into Textuality (memories, photographs, old drawings, and reports to be read and misread)—Textuality, and Desire—the desire, first, to fold the past over into the future and thus transcend mortality; second, to make the best of what *was* the best still of what *is*, and thus transcend judgment . . . neither of which can be done. The very theme of *rejuvenation*—who or what deserves it, and who or what does not, and how much—is laden with such deep cultural significance that restoration architects soon grow expert in handling the almost irrational political skirmishes that arise almost without fail with communities, landlords, and even other preservationists. Difference is the issue at every turn.

An old building restored "to its former glory," after all, is doubly glorious; once because it was (probably) indeed a good building and, cleaned, we can see that now, but once again because, transposed through time into its new, modern *context,* we encounter that context reflected as *decadent* and, by a curious reversal, old. The "old" building is miraculously unsullied by time. We reject the new but not the renewed, while the authentically new, i.e., the modern, stands rebuked.

And yet, we wonder, is the restored building somehow false, like an old lady saved from the grave, caked in make-up, and propped from behind? Is she not too bright? Was the old building ever like this? Where are the shortcuts, the simulacra, the electric fixes? Where is the air conditioning tucked? "The handrail is original, but the wallpaper was specially recreated from old photographs. Here you can see the smoke marks of the 1867 fire; they decided to leave that. Those doors were actually salvaged from the Criterion Building down the street, you know, the one they took down last year, with the columns. But they fit in well here." And so on.

As evidenced in this imagined yet typical snippet of conversation, authentic/inauthentic is the opposition posed everywhere. And it is unresolvable. Reconstruction, one might say, involves Deconstruction.[59] Among members of the architectural profession, practitioners of preservation and restoration are perhaps the most practical, earnest, and non-theoretically minded. And yet it is they, through the play of some of the most subtle systems of differences, deferrals, and differings in the architectural enterprise, who work closest of all to the production of theater, memory, and meaning.

4. ITERABILITY AND MEANING

The reader may have noticed that my presentation so far has all but omitted treatment of the relationship of a building to its physical, social, or historical context. This is because Deconstruction, as a rule, proceeds from an essentially conservative definition of what the *work* at hand is, and limits its actions to what is *internal* to the work.

At first this may seem an unwise and unnecessary stratagem. Certainly it distinguishes itself from, and discounts *pari passu* almost all the modes of criticism which are launched and concluded not from within the work but from without.[60] For Deconstruction, to go very far outside the text (or circle of specific texts), say, to issues of the social milieu in which it is read now, or was written then, or to the life of the writer, to myth, or even the history of ideas, is to redefine the work-to-be-deconstructed as something larger: the *system* that is the book, the reader, the writer, the library, the culture, the structure and history of these, individually and then all together. But where does one stop? Context is endless; and wherever one draws the line one is vulnerable to the criticism that the context beyond that line has not been taken into account.[61] Deconstruction aims to show how the logic of the text is constituted anatomically, how its *meanings* are organized within its *means,* as it were, not because there is, or was, no outside causal influence on the text that could be looked at as such, but because the outside has already left its traces within! Thus Derrida's insistence on an internal, somewhat hermetic view. Deconstruction, implicitly, is a sort of self-deconstruction witnessed. Because *différance* "happens" everywhere, we can watch it happen within the most conventional and smallest of boundaries, such as the covers of a book, the walls of a building, the vocabulary of a language, or the terms and lines of an argument,[62] and if Derrida would deconstruct the "whole Western metaphysical tradition," he does it by implication *from* that part of the fabric he examines deconstructively. Within this ambit we are apt to find all that we need of the structure and material of the "outside world," sampled, referred to, reflected, re-used, and embodied almost holographically.[63]

In part, this fact is what troubles us about Deconstructivist architects whose "deconstructions" are posed as being of the *city.* Coop Himmelblau's work, for example, is an explicit reaction to Viennese *gemütlichkeit.*[64] Bernard Tschumi, Daniel Libeskind, and sometimes Peter Eisenman also share this strongly urbanistic orientation. We are troubled, because to deconstruct the *city* (as though one could!) by building a little building that ignores, challenges, or creatively misrepresents its surroundings is too easy by far. One might as well deconstruct an elephant with a flea, or Plato with a paragraph. To make matters worse, with a little terminological sophistry, any transgression of building codes, lot lines, building height, typical color, material, style—*any* unusualness—can be seen as "deconstructing" the urban norm conveniently displayed nearby. With this, however, much of what is useful and interesting about Derrida's Deconstruction for architects is translated into a sort of bad-boyism, a hit-and-run architecture of perpetration. The more difficult and more interesting project is for a building to be *almost* perfectly contextual, a viable *graft* onto and into the fabric of the city, and one that contains within itself its own best challenge to itself, and by implication all buildings in the urban fabric. Now life at large is mirrored, and the window to the eternal play of *différance* is opened at the heart.[65] We are almost ready to move on to the theme of iterability.

If a building is but a repetition of its neighbors, it mirrors them, thus containing and representing them. Now, whatever critical acts it performs also, it performs by implication to all. When a building is wholly different from its context, it disqualifies itself from the critical act before it has begun. The same applies to repetitions within the building in the context of its self-deconstruction. To understand this better, we must look into the interdependent nature of repetition and meaning, or in Derrida's terms, of *iterability* and meaning.

Let me begin with an argument which is my own, but which

Coop Himmelblau, Attic Conversion, Vienna, 1988.

intersects with Derrida's in many places and ultimately, I believe, converges with his.

If we repeat any word or phrase over and over, it loses its meaning. This we all know. If we repeat nothing, however—no sentence, no word, no phoneme—though utterance remains physically possible, it is just as incapable of bearing meaning as repetition *ad absurdum.* Let me try to demonstrate why this is so.

The nature of language is such as to permit the production of new sentences indefinitely by the partially rule-bound permutation of words. Words themselves, however, to be "words" and to function as words, have to sound much the same with each utterance of them, and have to be adaptable and reusable in a large variety of contexts (i.e., sentences). The meaning of a word depends on this "iterability," this capacity to be repeated.[66] The stability of its denotation- and connotation-sets, and its recognizability as the "same word," supports the very enterprise of permutatory sentence building.

Now, going forward one step, the same can be said of whole classes of sentences, such as descriptions, commands, questions, promises. Each of these has a characteristic grammatological, phonetic *form* superadded to its more or less unique selection of words, an iterable form that ensures its functionality as a unit of meaning in different contexts. Again, iterability is preconditional to meaning. This iterability, says Derrida, extends to quotations, dramatic performances, rehearsals, commentaries, jokes, puns, framings and bracketings-without-end, the very possibility of which, far from undermining or cheapening the serious, first, or unique utterance of the words, makes such un-framed seriousness itself possible.

But let us imagine that this were not the case, that no phoneme, word, phrase, sentence, ever need be repeated in a different context. Utterances would be entirely and foundationally unique to the situation in which they are uttered, at all levels of analysis. They would simply be natural, sonic outcomes of the mechanics of reality, a wail and rush, squeaking and throbbing, a *musique concret,* without a figure recognizable from anything else. Such a stream of "data" can refer only to itself; speaking loosely, it can be its own proper name. But, more precisely, it cannot truly *refer* at all. This is not to say that the stream has no structure, but that its structure is not one shared with any other phenomenon.

This being the case, it cannot be associated with any other phenomenon in any definite act of reference. Nor can it be appropriated by re-production. Therefore, it cannot be used as language.

Another tack, and then I will return to architecture.

Sounds made by nature, including most animal utterances, are involuntary. That is to say, they are not made purposefully, in order to convey a meaning (although, importantly, they may *be* meaningful to certain other animals). Rather, they are "sonic outcomes" like the ones I mentioned above, or they are spontaneous expressions of inner states such as alarm, anger, hunger, or desire. As effective as they are in group function, no one is *in command* of the voice. But how do we know this? The only criterion, ironically, is the selective use of *deception*, especially in conjunction with *mimicry*.[67]

Imagine a troop of proto-humans, named (by us) Abe, Beth, Camille, and Dereck. Now before and without language, they involuntarily make similar, species-specific utterances in certain situations; similar but not identical because of differences between them in age, sex, physique, and temperament. Abe sounds like Abe to the others, Beth like Beth, and so on. Two kinds of thing can happen, at first quite accidentally.

(1) We can imagine that the group is eating. Perhaps tired, perhaps confused or just playful, Camille voices the "wrong utterance" for the situation, say one normally elicited by the presence of snakes. The others respond to her vocalization anyway, turning to look upward. Camille sees and then seizes the advantage: she picks up the last passion fruit and eats it quickly. An amazing thing has happened. An utterance has been displaced, as it were, from context A to context B; re-produced, it has preserved its effect, and *in* its effect, it has taken on *meaning*. Camille has "heard herself speak" for the first time, and if she does it *again*, she has brought intention, reference, and language together into the world with one swoop.[68]

(2) Dereck is the largest fellow. He always gets his way, especially with food, but more especially with Beth and Camille. Abe finds that he can mimic Dereck's gruff voice, and does so one day when Dereck is gone. Beth and Camille think (to put words in their mouths somewhat prematurely): "that's not Dereck; that's Abe 'doing' Dereck. But maybe he means it, or has *become* Dereck." Disturbed, perhaps,

their behavior nonetheless adjusts itself to Abe's advantage. Once again deception, this time based on mimicry, constitutes a displacement, a re-usable use of an utterance "out of context," a displacement that in its functionality lends not only evolutionary fitness to the individual capitalizing upon it, but group fitness to the group that permits and controls the proliferation of deceptions into the system of motivated utterances we call language.

The same logic can be applied to many other situations, and to other expressive systems become sign-systems, such as gestures and inscriptions, especially in their earliest phases of development. "Semiotics," writes Umberto Eco, "is in principle the discipline studying everything which can be used in order to tell a lie. If something cannot be used to tell a lie, conversely it cannot be used to tell a truth."[69] Nor, we might add, can it be used to "tell" at all. Derrida presses the point, seemingly beyond language, thus:

> . . .[I]n the presence of its identity and in the identity of its presence, [a statement] is doubled as soon as it appears, as soon as it presents itself. It appears, in its essence, as the possibility of its own most proper non-truth, or its pseudo-truth reflected in the icon, the phantasm, or the simulacrum. What is is not what is, identical and identical to itself, unique, unless it adds to itself the possibility of being repeated as such. And its identity is hollowed out by that addition, withdraws itself in the supplement that presents it.[70]

But perhaps the most subtle and fundamental instance of the transformation of utterance into language, of involuntary expression into intentional referentiality, is the case of the repeated, *ineffectual* utterance. A dog barks at the presence of an intruder, a cat miaows because it is hungry, a baby cries in loneliness or discomfort . . . all these will continue as long as the stimulus is present and as long as there is energy enough to voice the pattern. Intentionality is unnecessary. But anyone who has owned a dog or a cat, or who has raised a baby, compellingly intuits that at some point each repetition of the utterance "quotes" or "cites" the one before, reinforcing it, insisting upon it *as a message*. The animal or child seems to be saying: "Get it?, Get it!?" Iteration not only begets what J. L. Austin called "illocutionary force," but establishes the utterance as linguistically meaningful because it is intentional in its reference to the previous instance.[71]

Why this interest in how *language* means when what we want to talk about is how *architecture* means?

One must be extremely wary of jumping to the still fashionable answer: "because architecture is a language." Architecture is not a language.[72] The best one can say is that, as bearers of meaning (whatever that means, exactly), architecture and language share certain common roots. Where? In the depths of evolutionary history. The mechanisms of iteration operate at just such a "root level" and, like most evolutionary achievements, have become structural to the meaning-texture of all present "moments of moment," be they now literary or architectural.

Let us then examine, in architectural terms, repetition and the capacity for repetition (exercised or not) that Derrida calls "iterability."

Clearly, most architecture is replete with repeated elements, from bricks, tiles, windows, roof beams, and columns, to geometrical figures, ornamental pieces, and abstract formal relationships. Indeed—and without recourse to a discussion of prefabrication (as interesting an idea as it becomes here), or style—one can assert that architecture is hardly *possible*, practically or physically, without the extensive repetition of material components, geometrical configurations, and cyclical acts of fabrication. But if, as I argue, it is not legitimate to equate such repeatables with words and thus succumb to the temptation of devising a linguistic theory of architectural meaning, where does one go next? I offer a few observations and directions. These continue to depart from those portions of Derrida's argument that seem to indicate that iteration undermines rather than supports intentionality, loosening the subject from his attachment to the world.[73]

It often happens at the drawing board that a designer must invent a unique configuration of materials, surfaces, edges, components, hinges, cuts, etc., in order to accommodate some singular function or to solve some unusual problem. But alone, he sees, the design solution looks odd; it will be construed, he fears, as a mistake, or as a sign of the limitations of his design method and vocabulary. Intuitively, he seeks an opportunity to "do it" again, to repeat the figure in other circumstances, perhaps to re-envision the entire design problem so that what *was* formerly unique is now seen as *systematic* in some sense, endemic and essential to his style—his very means of production—rather than accidental or imported. Put simply: by repetition he seeks to convey intentionality.[74]

Notice, however, that for the (once-unique) configuration to be seen as *meaningful* it cannot seem automatic or reflexive, a given given the situation, nor too molded by its context. Thus the importance of subtle *misuse* in thematizing a form or figure. By duplicating and displacing it against a heterogeneous background, by under-adapting it to the contexts of its re-appearances, by hinting at—flirting with— unnaturalness and nonfunctionality, it becomes, first, an "it," a "figure," at all, and then also the carrier of unspecified significance. Why else the insistence?[75]

Of course, not all repeated forms are proliferations of some singular problem solution, at least not in the day-to-day design of buildings. Although one could argue, I think cogently, that all iterated elements of architecture were *once* unique solutions to unique problems and thus non-significant in themselves except insofar as they were recognized *as* iterable, the thematized figures of a developed architecture such as ours are simply a part of the architect's *repertoire.*[76] The architect brings his repertoire of formal "solutions" to the design problem at hand not only from outside the problem, but from inside his own practice and from inside the discipline of architecture that he has studied. If one looks at the drawings done in an architect's office during a period, say, of two years, one is apt to find similar features in all the projects. Certain, perhaps novel, configurations of architectural elements are repeated. We say they are "under investigation," that the architect is exploring a certain "theme." Experiencing any one building first hand you may see myriad repetitions presented, and many themes, but *this* one, the one reappearing through different buildings, you do not.[77] It takes the perspective of a historian, a theorist, or the architect himself to look at the *oeuvre* of a period synchronically. To the iterations he discovers between different projects, meaning of a sort adheres almost automatically. Simply by virtue of *their* iteration (and then his dissemination of them in talk and books), significance is established.

Similarly, the design process itself is one of iteration over time. Those configurations which survive, or are held on to, from the first to the final design gain their weight in meaning in good part by virtue of that very survival, as though reappearance itself certified significance.

The possibility for thematization inheres in iterability. The multitude of architectural questions that flow from this Derridean formulation, if not wholly new, are painted anew. One example: If inimitable style is a contradiction in terms, then why and when should we complain about "imitators"? Another: Was not postmodernism's pastiche play with representations of the elements of classical architecture and with the icons of popular culture justified as meaningful by appeal to the iterability and referentiality of words and signs?[78] We shall look at a very few more examples, but first we should note that with all my talk of "meaning" and "significance" in these past paragraphs, I have not specified *what* the meanings are, or *wherein* the significance lies.

The fault lies not in my failure be specific—to examine a specific building, say—but in the nature of the "theory of iterability" itself. For iteration does not create meaning as much as its creates the *possibility* for meaning. The actual significance of repetitions through variable contexts is not, in and of itself, specifiable. Such "significance" is but a perfume, a promise vaguely made of actual meaning to come, a deferral. It merely announces the intentionality behind the order perceived. Iterations erect the structures behind and along which the actual, specific, and simpler *sense* of a work of architecture comes into being.[79]

The iterated figure in architecture is thus word-like (or phrase-like, or sentence-like) only inasmuch as it shares with the word the properties of recognizability as a unit, together with a certain lawfulness in the occasions of its appearance. But whereas the recognized word delivers us instantly to the image of the thing or idea or relationship for which it is its task in life to stand, the architectural figure, cast reluctantly into the role of a word, remains lost in the *promise* of so doing.

The power of spoken and written language lies in the precision with which words/signifiers are linked to referents/signifieds, and in its infinitely delicate tracing of some of the subtlest movements of thought. The precision is not perfect, to be sure, and to study the continual modifications and enfoldings of semantics by phonemical and "grammatological" structures is useful. If, however, "Derrida's central contention . . . that language is haunted by dispersal, absence, loss, the risk of unmeaning"[80] is justified, it is not because the subject is not in control, or because language is the mere by-product of *arche-writing*, as Derrida seems to claim, but because, looked at most closely, we must confront the fact that language is not the locus of meaning *anywhere*. Language merely stands in front of, and turns our mind to, that whose meaning must yet be fathomed. Language can no more stand accused, as it were, of "unmeaning," than it can take credit for "meaning."

Language is the proliferating crown of leaves and blossoms on a most ancient tree, a tree of meaning in whose lower regions only do we find the slower, steadier movements of architecture. Above, each leaf scintillates among the others, colored and coloring, reflected and reflecting, in ever changing groupings. Immediately below, the twigs and branches weave their own less intricate passage.

A tree is something grown, and there was meaning in the world long before spoken and written language evolved. Where? In the life lived by the billions of creatures who for millions of years regarded each other and the shape of their world with circumspection, with anticipation, or dread. Language is the outcome, the flowering, of such imports, such encounters between creature and creature, and creature and world. It bears the traces of all this in its structure, and depends continually on the connection for the sustenance of its meaning. At the risk of taking the tree metaphor too far (it is not one I will adopt for good), we might say that Derrida, located high within the tree, looks only *up* and *out*. "The thickness of the text," he says from amidst leaves,

> . . . *thus opens upon the beyond of a whole, the nothing or the absolute outside, through which its depth is at once null and infinite—infinite in that each of its layers harbors another layer.*[81]

He will not look *down*.

But, of course, he does; all the time, and without pointing it out. I alluded to this in the Introduction, at the outset of my presentation. Their moral tone aside, Derrida's metaphors are rich in evolutionary and ecologically sonorous content: his "tissues," his "scissions," his "invasions," his "consecrations," his "taking leaves" and "bolsterings," "underminings" and "expulsions," "plays" and "horizons," and his "circling bird(s)" that "rise up [from the mute text] and remove [their] point at the very instant [they] jab,"[82] . . . one could go on indefinitely with such examples. Like Freud, like Nietzsche, like the rest of us, he cannot speak without such evocations.[83] The true meaningfulness of metaphysical texts often lies not in the metaphysical claims and conclusions as such, nor in their logic, but in the movement, the viscerality, of the metaphors they seem merely to "employ" for explanation. The very essence and source of the meaning (Derrida squirms here) is the image pictured in/of/by the metaphor. We witness *it* rather than the text. If Deconstruction teaches us anything, it teaches us this. "Metaphor is never innocent," Derrida writes. "It orients and fixes results."[84] So Derrida's suppression of the natural grounding and the structure of his—and all—metaphoricity is all the more poignant: for he denies and denies again any rootedness to language while releasing from between the very warp and woof of text-as-such, and about text-as-such, some of the most beautiful, deeply resonant images of living, betrayal, pain, and transcendence since the Kabbalah.

Now it is well beyond the scope of this study to offer a complete and viable theory of architectural meaning. However, consideration of the force of iteration brings us to where we must offer something, or be silent about the Kimbell. It will be sufficient for our purposes here to appropriate and develop a little the Platonic view of meaning as dependent on *mimesis* (as did Quatremere de Quincy, applying it to architecture, in the early 19th century).

Architecture does not bear its meaning primarily by conventional and arbitrary association of signifiers with signifieds as does language, but by re-creating, re-collecting, re-constructing and re-producing the structures of the vital settings and situations of our primeval past. For, neglected only consciously, the traces of this history-before-history still reside in the mind's core, in the physical world, and in the movements of our language. It informs and energizes every meaningful image with the *eidos,* the logical structure, of living always.[85] This mimesis architecture carries out not literally, as might a play or an archeological text, but figuratively, or better, *figurally.* The vital iteration involved is thus not the "horizontal" one, between this figure before me and that same figure before me just a moment ago on the surface of the text/building, but a "vertical," interior one, between the form now and—within it and below it like a shadow on water—the form *then,* long gone but still present, still in-forming, still traced in my body, in the air, in my sleepiness, in the waves that rush ashore. I am describing a history that lives, and that we do not need reminding of because we are its outcome in every fiber. Let me enlarge.

In *Glas* and *On Grammatology*, Derrida proposes that the history of writing is also a theory of writing, and that both must shade away indefinitely to a time, a logical region, where writing always was and is: *arche-writing*. Similarly, it is instructive to recall that all of Architecture, which we usually take to begin in earnest some nine thousand years B.C.,[86] represents no more than one five-hundredth of the time we know man has been on the earth and one millionth of the time mammals have been extant. During this seminal period, the essential elements of advantage accorded by certain patterns—figures—of shelter construction and site selection were becoming a part of *all* living and surviving: temperature control, defensibility, proximity to food sources and fresh water, armor, view and privacy, identity and social activity support, and so on. And the sensibilities that give meaning to architecture are older still. One cannot help being awed at how many of what we take to be specifically modern problems emerge with general form intact from this unimaginably long terrestrial history of perception, consciousness, hunger, mobility, sexuality, desire, and fear. Paths of pursuit, places of surveillance, concavities for shelter, locations of food; traps, strongholds, graves . . . these, like drought and flood, are ecological givens common to all living things. Given too, and simultaneously, are the significance of high places and low places, light places and dark places, near places and distant ones, of inside and outside, cold and warm, soft and hard, easy to traverse and difficult to traverse, fertile and infertile, fresh and foul; of places bustling with others and places devoid of competition, or company, or one's own kind. The meanings of these places, far from "culturally assigned" or free for the invention, are givens for animals no less than for people; givens, for all intents and purposes, no less reliable than any natural physical law.

And now add to this the structured, sacred uses of architecture that accompanied civilization. Add the everyday scenes of the Bible, those settings of the first stories we hear—Rebecca at the well, the garden of Gethsemane, the walls of Jerusalem, the court of the Temple, the Sea of Galilee, or the visions of the book of Revelation—and look at their enormous evocative power in the West. If one stopped the historical narrative right here, a major part of the meaningfulness we unconsciously attach to places and to buildings today would be accounted for. But there is more, and closer by: the institutional structures of Western civilization, the history of our particular nation and community, the shapes of our individual lives up to the moment we are confronted by the moment, for example. And beneath it all, there is yet more—the dynamics of the purely physical world, and beneath that, the order of Order itself: the logical and mathematical regularities at the very base of things, which seem to undergird the universe, and which emerge intact almost wherever we look. *All* of these are levels of evolutionary history, whose "trace energies" continue to flow up into and through every moment we come to know better the implications, history, or workings of something—be it an act, an object, or a place. Meaning in-forms the moment. Meaning is thus not an object or something at rest that can be grasped once and for all: it is the very flow, and the very sensing of this flow, of in-formation.

The axis of this "vertical" or "inner-outer" dimension of flow, as distinct from the horizontal or surface dimension of purely textual iterations, I have elsewhere called the *dimension of depth*. And it is the recovery through figural mimesis of the deeper zones, layers, strata, on this vertical dimension that functions to bring meaning to what I have called "the moment of moment," the specious present at the "top," which, like a wave, like a moving convex lens, swells all that we regard thoughtfully with purport and fullness.[87]

In a mode (ironically) more Hegelian than Derridean, here Derrida's concept of iterability is seen as operating in a new dimension, namely the dimension of depth. *Différance*, interpreted in its first two senses as "difference" and then "delay/deferral," is now seen describing the necessarily timely nature of information actually in-forming. The play is one of levels. And the "iterable units" are not properly text or textual but, pre-linguistically, the vital settings and situations of our past. Our past, but not just of our rememberable past, such as the minutes before this one or our childhoods, but those of the childhood of Man, and of the earth. The dislocations, the regroundings, the re-contextualizations necessary to give iterations their figurality and significance are dislocations through time rather than space; they are repetitions and reiterations of deeply submerged patterns of habitation.

In fact, I would argue from all this that architecture began/begins not with the construction of shelter per se, nor the conscious creation of sacred places, but with the trans-position and preservation of certain patterns of shelter-making across different and inappropriate contexts—climatic, topographic, cultural—constituting, as Derrida would put it, a primary *writing* on/of the landscape.[88] In this deep way, architecture is always "against" its context, foreign to where it is, an im-position; a shifted, brought, re-deployed thing, still bearing the traces of exile and encampment.[89]

So the postmodernists were right: the meaning of architecture lies in the history of architecture. Their mistake was to look only a few hundred years back, and stop there. Their copying is ironic because it is guilty. Of what? Of superficiality and unoriginality. In other words, of adopting only the "face" of nearby things in place and history, and of shrinking from the twin journey to the origins of architecture, and to its possible destinies, for the source of form. The postmodernist lapse is not its use of collage, counterposition, irony, or even referentiality per se, but its obliviousness to the simultaneous co-presence in reality—disseminated—of the entirety of natural and cultural history in transparent, addressable strata. In *Complexity and Contradiction,* Robert Venturi over-reached with his frequent invocations of "levels of meaning." In fact, he discusses only the most conventional of symbolic meanings on the one hand, and, on the other, only compositional niceties of plan and elevation treatments. Providing nothing close to the close reading of individual works demanded by Deconstruction, he stopped far short too of identifying the "natural symbols within the conventional symbols of architecture," as Karsten Harries puts it.[90]

Traditional and vernacular architectures, we should note—so rich, so right, so rarely designed by those with Meaning on their minds—carry the entire course of their history within themselves, hiding their iterations *as* iterations by preserving their context so faithfully. This is how vernacular architecture escapes superficiality, but this is also, ironically, how it escapes "meaning" in the active sense, and remains silent. Unless and until the question of meaning is asked, its "iterabilia" and mismatches are not revealed.

What remains to account for? New work.

A new work of architecture is created self-consciously, as is any work of art, and, today, almost any public act or behavior. The fullness of a new work's meaning can be uncovered only by the deepest and not-strictly-Derridean of deconstructions, past the meanings put forward, and back through time to the beginning, down and down again through the levels of organization of life—from pure order at the "bottom" through physics, biology, human nature, our culture and the zone of personal history near the "top." For these strata actively underlie each passing moment, to this very one, now, delivering up meaning whether we like it or not, whether we know it or not. The artist, the writer, the architect of depth, is the person, the one, who feels called to taking a core sample of our existence, as it were, and to making the alignment of its sediments felt in his or her art. The artist reminds us of our home on earth, of what has been achieved, and of what is at risk.[91]

If all this is sounding more and more unmanageable in its vastness, and impossibly arcane to boot, then perhaps it is time to look at the Kimbell Art Museum, a deceptively simple building in which almost everything I have just said about meaning finds instantiation, along with every principle of Deconstruction.

C. DECONSTRUCTING THE KIMBELL

I have thus far selected, with Jonathan Culler's help, four principal themes of Deconstruction: (a) the (non!)concept of *différance,* (b) the process of hierarchy reversal, (c) the interplay of centers and margins, and (d) the function of iterability in the support and generation of meaning. Each, at different lengths, I have attempted to elucidate first in Derridean literary/philosophical terms, and then in terms of some well-known works of architecture. It would be ideal if we could now go back through these four themes, one by one, and identify the presence and play of each in the Kimbell Museum. Unfortunately this turns out to be difficult, not because the themes arc not there, in the building, to be seen and discussed, but because the experience of the building brings many of them into play simultaneously, here, there, and overall. I propose therefore to discuss the building in its own aspects, in a series of short sub-essays— or assays—arranged in no especially significant order. Our principles will be brought into play by turns, as they are illuminating.

The Kimbell Art Museum is a landmark work in Louis Kahn's oeuvre and has established its place in the history of modern American architecture. Since it is thus well known to students of architecture ("students" in the largest sense), I will dispense with any organized, neutral description of the building. I will also assume that the reader is reasonably familiar with Kahn's major projects as well as with the general character of the Kimbell, its context, and its program. If

Fort Worth, aerial view with the Kimbell Art Museum.

the reader has *visited* the Kimbell Art Museum, so very much the better.[92]

One more prefatory remark. Kahn was a skilled listener and collaborator, a modest man who felt himself to be in the service of something larger. Many of the crucial refinements[93] we find in his buildings were the work of his assistants, such as Marshall Meyers, his consultants (typically Edison Price and Richard Kelly, lighting, and George Patton, landscape), or his contractor (Thomas S. Byrne, Inc. at the Kimbell); and for the greater part of his career, Kahn relied on August Komendant for critical engineering insight. Kahn's high-mindedness held these men together, surely, but it also attracted a series of *clients* who joined him in his quest for an adequate offering to the "spirit that is Architecture," in fact, for a *metaphysical architecture,* parallel in ambition to any metaphysical text advanced by a philosopher. (This very "metaphysicality" is what suggests the kind of Deconstructionist analysis of Kahn's work in general that we attempt here with the Kimbell.) Each client (at the Kimbell, Richard Brown), in his own way inspired, expected, taxed, and allowed Kahn to pursue his vision. To that extent, each deserves to take some credit for what excellence and complexity we find in Kahn's (especially later) work. Therefore, if in what follows we find too much "remarkableness," we should remember that a paean to Louis Kahn's specific genius or omniscience is neither intended nor warranted. And if, by the lights of conventional wisdom, we will be reading things into the building that "really aren't there"—especially Deconstructionist things—we do not have to believe that Kahn *intended* them all or was in command of them all. Beginning with the many operations endemic to the architectural project as such, and ending with the marks of the deeper motions, frictions, and contradictions in Kahn's thought specifically, the Kimbell stands with all buildings as a complex trace of many incidents, many contributions, and many confrontations.[94] Indeed this richness is what makes the critical deconstruction of almost any building possible.

1. THE PLAN OF THE BUILDING

Here we consider the overall plan, or *parti,* of the Kimbell, as it can be appreciated from the outside or from the air. At this level of analysis, already, the plan of the Kimbell can be read in two contrasting ways.

The first reading. If we look at the "footprint" (that is, the outline inscription of the building on the ground) and ignore the rest, we see the form of a very classical, Beaux-Arts plan: axial symmetry, with the axis of symmetry passing through front and rear entrances, a central reception/orientation zone with a minor cross-axial stair from a lower level within. Wings to each side embrace the approach, with open porticos along these and before the entrance, and there is a central plaza with symmetrically disposed pools. The dominant east-west axis extends across the site to cross at right angles a larger north-south axis emanating from the older Will Rogers Memorial Center. The row of trees that form a soft screen in front of the Kimbell actually constitute the eastern part of the older *allée,* to the Will Rogers Memorial Center, the western part of which is now occupied by a street but still visible. To use the trees the way Kahn did for *his* project constitutes an appropriation of, indeed a *grafting* onto, in Derridean terms, the earlier system. More will be offered about the site design specifically in the next section; the point here is to note the axial, hierarchical nature of the plan, and its extension, by grafting, of the axiality of a prior structure.

The second reading. Now we look a little closer at how

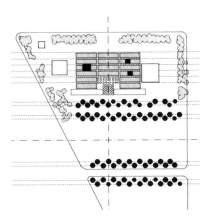

The Kimbell, site plan with major axes and trees.

the plan is rendered in fact. We see no central domes, no *allées*, no tile-roofed wings, no window openings, no colonnaded porticos, no resolution of facades . . . all of which are called for by the *parti;* instead, a banal repetition of ribs, the "barrel vaults," cut as though from an indefinitely large bolt of ribbed fabric. We find a classical, centered, closed and terminalizing outline (reading 1) filled in by a modern, nakedly repetitive, interminable and open medium (reading 2). A deeper theme is announced than that of some dialogue between periods of architecture, the Classical and the Modern. Here the problem of the One and the Many—that deepest of metaphysical themes—is brought into action and left intentionally unresolved by any larger and reconciliatory act. Instead of "amounting to something," stating a theme and developing it to a climax, the building repeats its elements without comment, in uncompromising parallelism.

And then, instead of shaping the building nicely shaped around courtyards, from the air we see the three courtyards dropped into the structure like punch-outs, or notes on a stave of aleatory music.[95]

One senses these contradictions palpably when on the ground, around and within the structure. From the Beaux-Arts plan of this small building, Kahn draws out the air of calmness, dignity, knowingness, and permanence that befit an institution (Kahn would often capitalize this word) such as the Museum. And yet, undermining this "air" in one sense but accentuating it in another, there is the almost violent shearing-off of the vault-ends north and south, and the arbitrary numerosity, launching, and terminating of the vault sequence east and west. Both of these last gestures suggest a largeness and a systematicity that go beyond the confines of *this* museum, together with a kind of practical dumbness, almost an insensitivity, to "composition" quite at odds with

The Kimbell, view from the north.

the sensitive deliberations, crownings, and culminations of the classical ideal. Thus one enters not a prearranged, prescribed hierarchy of spaces, but a single field, modulated and punctuated here and there by programmatic events. Correspondingly, the explicit valorizations of which the classical idiom is so capable are sublimated and transposed into a system of marks, gestures, and positionings in the field that is far, far subtler, as we shall see.

Such esoteric and high-minded stuff! But origins—and real motivations—are often more humble and pragmatic, as we began to suggest in the preceding paragraph by noting the plan's "dumbness." The building *section,* we learn, was conceived of and developed long before the *plan* was settled. In itself, this is an irrelevant fact. To detect its significance in terms of our discussion, let us listen to Marshall Meyers:

[Kahn] thought of it as a section through a gallery and as the element of the building, in a way complete to itself in that it housed the light, air and power and correct dimension for viewing the art. It could be repeated as necessary and it could be longer or shorter. [Richard] Brown [the client] was quick to see the advantage of this because of his earlier problems in Los Angeles. If the budget required this museum plan to reduce in size, it could be done without tampering with the critical viewing dimensions. . . . Many of the early schemes of the building demonstrate this potential: more or less elements, variations in their composition, and variations in their length.[96]

In addition, Brown was not certain of the eventual size and nature of the collection, only of the limits of the size of the artworks. The open-endedness, the systematicity, the gener-

The Kimbell, schematic section looking north.

ality, and the iterability (more about which later) of the gallery vault section was thus a programmatic necessity, quite in keeping with the unapologetic iterability and modularity typical of factories, warehouse rows, or grain silos, in a word, of the most pragmatic genres of architecture.[97] (It is the frankness of this logic that makes the Kimbell a building that invites being added to by repetition without fear of defilement or de-formation, as indeed architect Romaldo Giurgola and the museum's administrators had determined to do in 1989.[98])

On a more abstract plane again: Louis Kahn was Beaux-Arts trained, and haunted by monistic ideals.[99] Almost all his public buildings were highly symmetrical, centered, and axial in plan, exploring themes of concentricity and hierarchy. One cannot help imputing that Kahn was uncomfortable if not incapable of designing major buildings any other way. *Order* was what he had sought and found in emulating the symmetry and hierarchical resolutions of classical Roman models.[100] Until the Kimbell.

In the plan of the Kimbell we see a movement, begun with the Salk Institute and continued at the Mellon Center for British Art and Studies at Yale,[101] in which two families of "forces" come finally into full oppositional play. We see hierarchy both stated and erased, infinitude declared and delimited, specificity pursued and then generalized. The principal themes of Classicism and Modernism are locked in against each other, and the timeless, upright pleasures of pragmatism both embraced and leapt over laughing. We see a coincidence of contrary images—contrary in kind, in ambition, and in structure, and not unlike those of Thoreau in *Walden Pond* (discussed earlier in this essay)—two metaphors about the truth of things, at war, perhaps, within Kahn. Certainly they are unreconciled logically. Yet they produce, with the *frisson* of their synergy, both the possibility of a larger meaning that neither figure could contain, as well as the physically largest statement of a fundamental opposition. Fundamental? According to Deconstruction, an opposition manifested at any level is something we cannot declare as either originary or derived, but only as *disseminated* to all elements of the work's composition and tectonics. Very well.

All this Kahn achieves with a boldness and economy of formal invention that we have yet to appreciate fully.[102]

2. THE SITE

The site for the Kimbell was a difficult one: a large, asymmetrically trapezoidal lot west of downtown Forth Worth, evenly and markedly sloped down toward the east, the upper part of which is transversely crossed by the central axis of the Will Rogers Memorial Center, as I have mentioned. This axis posed no difficulty—so tenuous is (and was) its presence "on the ground." The site was quite large enough for the program, the slope gentle, and the soil good. Then wherein lay the difficulty?

I think Kahn's response confirms my belief that the primary difficulty lay in the slope itself. A gentle but persistent slope on a large (water-permeable) area of land presents no special technical problems to an architect. But an architect sensitive to *ch'i* must make a considered response. *Ch'i* is a Chinese term meaning "spirit-energy," used by ancient (and modern) geomancers to describe the "spatial forces," good and bad, created by a building or land form. Like an immaterial, compressible fluid, *ch'i* flows smoothly or roughly, strongly or weakly, around, along, over and under things, and finally through us, affecting our well-being and good fortune. In order to create harmonious places, thus, one must treat *ch'i* with due regard to its action, its "will" and "composure." In all, the workings of *ch'i* are elaborate in their manifestations and consequences, forming the basis of the art of *feng shui.* [103]

Now Kahn may or may not have known about *ch'i* as such, but he could feel that on a wide and consistent slope, visual stability is threatened. Like dishes on a tilted table, buildings tend to slide. The verticality of verticals is threatened as the inclined "local horizon" appropriates the true one. Space itself, *ch'i*, seems to flow down the hill in a broad wash, unresisted, persistent, carrying with it not only objects (visually/kinesthetically speaking, of course) but our gaze, our line of regard.

Now, the architect may respond in a number of ways in order to achieve the necessary stability: with emphatic cutting and filling, with powerfully heavy and vertical forms, and/or with roof lines and other significant contours adopting an opposing and thus neutralizing stance, and so forth. Kahn chose to build a *dam* of sorts to both receive and reverse the tide of space, and a *valley,* to stabilize the slope. The Kimbell is a low building extending over much of the lower width of the site. In section one can see how the building stops the flow of *ch'i*, "correcting" the slope, and forming, with this damming action, a virtual valley across which the building now "looks back."

(Just up the hill at the Amon Carter Museum, Philip Johnson had taken the opposite approach. He had built a high, level platform, and upon it a pretentious structure facing—indeed possessing—the eastern view to downtown Fort Worth. Whereas the Kimbell ignores the city but embraces nature and Texas, the Amon Carter does the reverse. The Kimbell lies low, looking back and inwards, screened by trees from the west, and is happy, one imagines, to efface itself before the gaze of Johnson. In all, the Kahn building might easily be seen if not as a rebuke, then a reply, an opposition, to Johnson's Amon Carter and that for which he/it stands. But this is not of special interest.)

The flow of *ch'i* is corrected, stabilized, but still free. Good. Now what, in nature, does one find in valleys? Rivers and lakes—water flowing, collected, contained. At the Kimbell the pools are placed precisely at the new low point. And what, in nature, does one find next to water? Trees, and with trees, shade and rest. At the Kimbell, to the west of the ponds, are two rows of trees, given by the site but now appropriated by a new context; and to the east the porticos—that is, the open vaults of the building—rise up and bend over to the water too, like a row of willows. And there are benches in their shade. Kahn has re-created an ancient and Edenic scene—the tree-lined watercourse—one as stirring and rare in the plains of Texas today as it was in East Africa two million years ago; and this with the subtlest of mimetic gestures, without pictoriality, without literality, without compromising the tectonic discipline of architecture. Coming upon this scene is like hearing a song, an air, both strik-

The Kimbell, view from the west.

ingly new and inexplicably familiar. It seems intrinsically *right* and good to us, and meaningful in ways that underlie, and almost defy, speaking and writing about it.

But, we notice, the water is not still, like a pond or lake. Nor does it flow like a river. Were it to flow like a river, along its length, Kahn would have had to assign and contrive an "up river" and "down river" side. Were it at rest, we could not hear it; and had it had fountains (for the noise), the source would be questioned. Instead, Kahn has the water flowing quite *unnaturally* west to east, across the breadth, rushing across a weir. Why?

The impetus for this unnatural direction of flow is seen immediately: it is the sublimated, emerging-from-below, processional energy of the vaults. The last and open vault is "broken open." It spills itself forward. It arches up, as though tripping, billowed, and falls transmogrified into vanishing water, sound. In this narrative of causation, the direction of the flow of water tells us about the *ch'i* direction of the building in general, how the site's downward rushing *ch'i* is opposed and cancelled. It tells us in which direction the repeating vaults are to be "read," and how the *mass* of the building, now seen to begin on the east so abruptly and loudly, is dispersed into space, burst, to deposit its remains at our feet in quietness.

Kahn would not stay with the natural alone. This would be meaningless iteration, the creation of nice places with nice trees and nice pools, which, as it approached true naturalness, would not only lose the figurality of an intentional iteration, but lose the range of meaning levels collected in its re-collection. It is from *différance* that the animus of meaning is born, and this Kahn seemed to know. Without perversity of a sort, without including and abrading levels of order from the natural down to the purely geometrical and from the pragmatic up to the mystic, meaning could not emerge, stepping out, as it were, from behind the simple facticity of presence. But, perhaps more importantly, without re-producing the deep structure of an archaic environment *and* turning away from it at the last moment, withdrawing, leaving opportunities for its crossing out and contradiction . . . meaning could also not emerge. We fall short of, we fall away from, the expected unaffectedness of the natural, ideal archetype knowingly, all the better to evoke its presence in loss. We reveal its contours in a formal mime that avoids the inauthenticity of a self-aware, cultured naturalness or primitivism and an impossible literality. And we must wittingly leave the tools behind, too, for our deconstruction.

Besides, if breaches are inevitably left over in any attempt to encompass the unencompassable—to "give measure to the immeasurable" as Kahn would say—then it becomes important that those breaches, themselves now a system of marks, be aligned in the direction of the effort; aligned like so many fingers pointed at the moon but which point at the same time, and no less, to the hand and to the pointer.

3. THE VAULTS, CONSIDERED INDIVIDUALLY

The poured-in-place concrete "vault," 100 feet long, 23 feet wide, and 20 feet high (springing from 12 feet 6 inches), is the most obvious unit of iteration at the Kimbell.[104] A remarkable invention in itself, it has received much attention from architectural critics and teachers over the years.

Perhaps most widely appreciated are two facts: one, that the vault is not really, i.e., structurally, a continuous arch or "barrel vault" resting, here, on longitudinal beams, but a concrete *shell*, a beam itself, with considerable post-tensioned steel reinforcement along its curved length; and two, that the vault in some way addresses, imitates, "means," the vault of the sky. It is also well known that the curve is a rather special one mathematically: a cycloid, rather than an ellipse or semicircle.

A closer look reveals more.

First, the effect. Most clearly appreciated in the two open porticos, the sheer delicacy, span, and loft of these vaults is instantly impressive. They seem to float almost unnaturally,

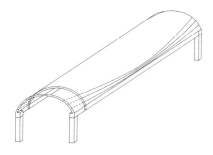

The Kimbell, typical vault reinforcement.

lofted by . . . one cannot say. The source of their strength is invisible. The columns are so slender, and, set impossibly far apart at the very corners, they deny the burden of their burden. Yet there is a pain here, a tension under the serenity and ease of the geometry both literal (the cables within), and phenomenal. Kahn, always interested in the nature of structural materials, is not content to use materials without asking something *of* them, without shaping them to express their inherent limits.[105] The result is paradoxical, or should one say tense? At the Kimbell as elsewhere in Kahn's work, materials are left natural. Wood, marble, concrete, cork, steel . . . these are cut, formed, and marked quite conventionally, sensibly, and sensitively, and their finishes are left open to view. Yet all are driven to extremes from behind, as it were, to new forms, greater spans, to unusual demands for precision construction in alignments, assembly, surfaces, flushness. One thinks of the cantilevered corners of the Richards Medical Research Buildings, the concrete arch ties at Ahmedabad, the stainless steel panels at the Mellon, the flush, honey-colored cabinetry at all these, and, of course, of our case in point, the concrete of the vaults still stained and shining from their pouring upon steel forms. One feels their "pain," yet witnesses their composure. One knows of their weight, but witnesses their levitation.[106]

A smaller observation: each vault-edge that does not drain onto a flat interstitial roof has a fully formed concrete gutter. A *gutter?* No afterthought this, no embarrassment, the gutter is large and integral, cast with the vault. It not only gives a good, visual, shadow-casting edge, in the Beaux-Arts tradition, but shows Kahn, in typical fashion, easily embracing the marginal and practical and bringing them both fully into the fold of an amplified system.

We move underneath a portico vault and look up. Each

The Kimbell, south portico.

vault has a "lip" at its end whose curvature does not match the cycloidal curvature of the vault-shell itself. Undoubtedly required by engineering considerations, we are unsure as to its precise function. We accept on faith—and it seems natural—that there be some stiffening at the ends of this thing! But we look at how the lip arrives on the column. There is a sort of a *block* which itself seems to belong to each and all of three elements: to the column as a minimalist capital; to the lip as a terminating, in-turning anchor; and to the curious expression of a *beam* along the entire length of the vault (apparently supporting it and a beam we know is not a beam at all in the conventional sense) as a sort of hook or ledge piece! What is more, the column is not centrally loaded: the weight of the vault comes down heavily on the outside third. We see no response/effect of this eccentricity on the column's shape, and this "block" now seems to negotiate the eccentricity problem at its source also. The "beam," the block, the lip, the gutter, all these are *parergonal* physically and in their reading of the nature of the vault, and yet without them the vault would be not only weaker but, visually, unvaulted.

But why all this mastery, this repression and ambiguity? The answer becomes clearer inside the building. Here we see the geometry released into a play of differences, a fully deployed system.

The vaults are many in number, and each must end (in their length) either definitively at the boundaries of the building or, within, "provisionally," defining themselves and permitting movement below at the same time. In both cases, a trialog of curves is produced: curve A, the cycloidal curve of the underside of the vault as it meets the lip; curve B, the elliptical curve of the bottom edge of the lip; and curve C, the

The Kimbell, exterior portico vault "block".

iterated cycloidal curve of the upper edge of the wall/infill panel. Glass is introduced into the difference between curves B and C, admitting light, but also in its brightness calling attention to the play of curvatures, to the difference itself, to the trace of the decision *not* to use an ellipse for the vault. After all, the presence of a *cycloid* is not witnessable unless we see it next to what it is almost, but is not, what it could easily have been, but isn't: namely, an ellipse.

Of course, other things are achieved too by this play of differences. The vaults are separated by seven feet to create service zones in the Kahnian taxonomic scheme of servant/served (a gesture we will remark upon again and more fully later). The introduction of these three curves at the cut-edge of each vault delineates a use and a context for the inside edge of the columns, for they form from the precise column-width—up, over, around and down—a structural "service zone" utterly consistent with the larger system of servant and served. The travertine veneer infill panel rests weightlessly, in fact improbably: it betrays no clipping or bracket support from the columns. The travertine here belongs uneasily to three realms: the served space over which it hovers, the ser-

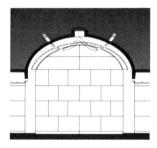

The Kimbell, interior elevation showing three curves.

The Kimbell, lobby looking north.

vant, or marginal space of transition between vaults of which it announces the beginning, and the end condition, the wall, in remnant.

What about this *cycloid?* Why not a common ellipse? Strength was not the issue.[107] Even granted that a semi-circular arc would rise too high, and a circular segment would look chopped off, an ellipse is only very subtly different from a cycloid. Was Kahn simply exercising the eye of a Designer, like the artist who steps back, squinting to determine whether he *likes* a curve? Perhaps. There are many cycloid curves, and Kahn surely had to choose among them with his "good eye" for proportion; but why a cycloid in the first place?

The cycloid is the curve traced in the air by a point on a rolling disc. The disc may roll on its edge like a penny, or on a side lip or drum smaller than the disc. The point that traces the curve may lie on the edge or may lie anywhere on the disc from the edge to the center. The relationship between the rolling surface diameter to the marker (point) position gives rise to a family of curves called cycloids. A familiar example might be the path traced at night by the reflector on a bicycle wheel.

I believe, but cannot prove, that the translatory motion inherent in the generation of the cycloid, a movement of tremendous logical depth because it is so purely mathematical, is precisely what Kahn hoped would surface in the perception of the vaults, energizing them with *ch'i*, vectorizing them in their row character, and guiding our attention to the further cycles, iterations, of rolling that could have been present but are not.[108] Linked by virtual, serial motion, the ensemble acts together.

Now we must move on to contemplate:

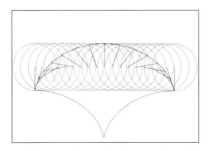

A cycloidal arch with its evolute.

4. THE VAULTS, CONSIDERED TOGETHER

The vaults roll, or let us say, they seem to move east and west gracefully enough. A diagram of the idea might look like the figure below. But wait. There is a seven-foot-wide gap between each of them, flat and square. This "rolling" is not continuous but interrupted, and these interruptions are drastic, even ugly, and unapologized for. How to explain this? Three ways, each less speculative than the one before it.[109]

If you watch a point on the circumference of a rolling wheel—and watch its motion carefully relative to the surface it is rolling on rather than the wheel as such—it descends rather awkwardly as it touches down, and seems to jerk too swiftly back up. There appears to be a slight hesitation, a sticking and then jumping action, hard to describe, but distinctly unnatural. Unnatural? Unnatural relative to our own musculature's notion, as it were, of what good movement looks/feels like, say walking or somersaulting. Now these problematic, dynamic, accelerative effects are not *present* in the static trace of a cycloid in a geometry book, say, or as built at the Kimbell where the cycloid is surely a graceful curve in itself; and, by rights, they might safely be ignored. But I think Kahn may have watched a rolling disc and felt that a *spacing* was needed, even in this rolling flow, precisely at the moment where the point seems to hesitate and gather its strength. The absent real motion was, he hoped and trusted, buried, compressed, into the cycloidal trace. For the later Kahn, we might remember, the ideal Platonic Form was never to be adopted directly and/or solely on its own authority, but to be brought up *through* human nature, human experience, and human ingenuity into the light of day and its moments of moment. Certainly the visual result at the Kimbell is the creation, across these pauses, of moments of

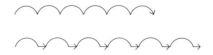

The Kimbell, "rolling" vaults.

submergence as in the stroke of a swimmer, moments of rest-in-motion as in the foot-fall of a walker, or of moments of punctuation as in closing one's eyes . . . the creation, in any case, of a good and pleasant "motion" not entirely explained by the above, and a continuous deferral of rest or arrival, a continous passing along and giving over of something inexplicable.[110]

In all, this first interpretation is a naturalistic one, close to an account that might be made with Theodore Lipps's concept of *einfühlung,* or "empathy." Derrida faces us in another direction. The horizontal seriality of the Kimbell vaults appears as some proto-*writing.* We do not have to believe in any encryption here, nor accept wholesale the linguistic analogy, to appropriate profitably Derrida's language about writing. Derrida, in any case, is not speaking only about everyday writing, but of an *"arche-writing"* whose structure makes language, in all of its manifestations, possible.[111]

Within the horizontality of spacing, which is in fact the precise dimension I have been speaking of so far, and which is not opposed to it as surface opposes depth, it is not even necessary to say that spacing cuts, drops, and causes to drop within the unconscious: the unconscious is nothing without this cadence and therefore without this caesura. This signification is formed only within the hollow of différance: of discontinuity and of discreteness, of the diversion and reserve of what does not appear.[112]

Read together "vocally," the vaults nonetheless must stand alone "written."

"On all levels of life's organization," continues Derrida in an unusually romantic and essentialist passage, "that is to say *of the economy of death* . . . [a]ll graphemes are of testamentary essence. And the original absence of the subject of writing is also the absence of the thing or referent."[113] The rolling motion is absent but presented, just as the Edenic place is absent but presented, and Kahn himself, the "writer," is absent but presented. We do not read between the lines or between the words for meaning, but it is because of these betweens that we can read; we have a speaker because of the absent thing, and writing because of the absent speaker.

Our third interpretation does not ignore these first two as much as build on them. The seven-foot gap between the

vaults begins a series of gaps and displacements in the dis-
position of the vaults throughout the whole building. It is a
system of ruptures, fissures, slits, omissions, withdrawals,
erasures, dis-junctions, "betweens," and separations numerous enough to delight any Deconstructivist's heart, a
system, not anarchic, but one that creates quite coolly and
regularly an all-but-perfect map of an intricate servant/
served economy.

Before listing and discussing the various separations, fissures, omissions, etc. in the next section, however, mention
needs to be made of what is perhaps the Kimbell's most obvious characteristic: the *repetition* of the vault as its clearest
and strongest formal statement. How does what we know
about "iterability" and meaning shed light on this?

From the outside, the repetition is marked and insistent. Earlier we spoke of the vault ensemble's open-endedness and
arbitrary truncation suggesting continuity in all directions,
and we spoke of the vaults' creation, within, of a neutral field
of space with movement both along and across the vaults'
north-south polarization. Now we look at our earlier for-
mula that "requires" that an iterated element not change in
itself, but appear in different contexts more or less identically.

Repeating some design element—say, a window, or door-
way or whole building—with changes to each, is, of course,
a common device used by architects to achieve the multi-
identity of variety together with the inherent economy of
repetition. Housing projects, small and large, urban and
suburban, are where one is mostly likely to see attempts being made by architects to "pre-personalize" units on this logic of repetition with variation; for generally, in any democratic system, providing the buildings' users with this
apparent opportunity to effect individuation is considered a
Good Thing. But what we are thinking about with iterability is a different, inverse logic. The principle of iterability goes
deeper than simple repetition, even repetition with variation, because *the that* which is iterable, which indeed iter-
ates, is always *the that* which is identical in each instance. A
word may be pronounced differently by many people, but
the word remains *that* word, and invariant, nuance notwithstanding. Thus the variation introduced by most architects—
Building A is blue with porches, Building B is red with shutters and decks, Building C is yellow with porches and arches,

to take a simple and mundane example—does not demonstrate iterability nor the kind of meanings to which iterability gives structure, except insofar as each building is located contextually, and differently, with respect to the others. If we really think about it, no amount of detail or color variation between otherwise identical buildings really satisfies; the kind of identity and personalization offered by such schemes is trivial by itself, and not really alleviated by increasing the variability.

Consider the alternative. When a living unit, say a town house, has a *position* on the block, a position relative to the others, a position with respect to the sun, a view, a tree, an intersection, and so on, then the question of identity is answered without the necessity of disguising the iteration. The Royal Crescent housing at Bath and Landsdown Crescent (by John Wood the Younger and John Palmer, respectively) are two canonical and early examples of the deferral of identity to the larger scale of the site. This they do by giving to each repeated unit a position defined clearly not just by distance or number or name, but "characterologically" and contextually by position and orientation to the compass points, to the town, to views, to a system of centers, axes, crowns and ends, and to a placement between garden and roof.[114]

This discussion has not carried us too far from the Kimbell and its iterated vaults. For, clearly, we have two ways to "read" this iteration. On the one hand, we might say that the vaults are identically repeated *except* for the western ones that have no skylight, except where they are interrupted by courtyards, except where they are omitted completely, ex-

John Wood the Younger, Royal Crescent Housing, Bath.

cept where the skylight is baffled closed (in the auditorium, where it appears uniquely also over a double-high space), and so on. Extending this, the space beneath each vault is open and isotropically repeated, *except:* where the functions vary, the partitions guide things, the light changes, and so on. On the other hand, one might say that no two vaults are really the same, that the variables just mentioned as well as the structural interruptions of the courtyards suffice to make each effectively an individual thing, a fragment of, or variation on, a *norm,* which is itself ambiguously defined (and we may choose): either an open portico vault or a closed vault with skylight.

Neither reading is mistaken. This is Kahn awaiting Deconstruction. Happily, the delineation of the vaults is such that the word "vault" has a clear denotation in the visible that-which-despite-variation-and-interruption-is-indeed-iterated, and happily too (for at one point in the design process the building had twice the number and length of vaults and no fewer than ten courts) the number and size of the vaults is such that, inside, most are visible in whole or part simultaneously, and *situated differently*. One vault is near the door, three are around the north court, four make the west wing, and so on. The building stops well short of actually creating the infinite and neutral space it promises it could. It gives us instead a recurring theme, the *vault-section*, over an articulated field of behaviors, movements, alignments, and illuminations, one that we can see as a whole and systemically variegated "background"—in other words, as iteration over against a changing context. Thus, while the vault-section's physical form extrudes and proliferates in a real horizontal dimension, there to meet this accident or that modification, the vault's purely iterable form—its sectional, abstract figure—is permitted to extend "down" into the region of traces, where its diagrammatic reproduction of the sky is no less original than the sky itself.

5. THE SYSTEM OF SEPARATIONS AND BETWEENS

First, in the north-south alignment along their lengths, each vault is pulled away from the next by three feet.

Second, in the east-west dimension, each vault is separated by the seven-foot zone we have been dwelling on so far.

Third, the three courtyards are subtractions from, and at the same time additions of, space to space.

Fourth, the shell of each vault is withdrawn a foot or so from the walls that enclose the interior—north and south walls, east and west walls—differently.

Fifth, the interior vaults are all centrally split open at the crown along their entire length.

Sixth, all conditioned air enters the interior through a vertical displacement of the metal-paneled service ducts from the vault "beams," creating a horizontal slit.

Seventh, outside, the water for the pools originates in (two) long, almost invisible cracks about six inches wide.

Eighth, back inside, the stairs between levels are narrow omissions, almost cave-ins in the floor, treated as fissures or chasms.

Ninth, the junction of no two materials on the same plane is treated other than with a recess. The same is true of all surfaces made of components, or in multiple stages.

Servant and served: this is the scheme restated in all these cases. Each bears looking at. (See pages 98 and 99.)

The first: by pulling the vaults away from each other by four feet (exterior dimension) a small amount of direct light and a considerable amount of reflected light enters the vault space from on high. The light "serves" the space's function, which is to show art, as well as the building's other function, which is to show itself. Below the vault, this same interval intersecting with the one next listed creates a pochéed void for

The Kimbell, vaults withdrawn four feet.

the air conditioning riser ducts to serve the galleries. Where it does not do this, the pulling apart allows light into the vertical fissure between the vaulted spaces; for example, notice the curtain-wall glazing of the library vault end walls, facing directly the blank wall of the adjacent vaults, and notice the effective introduction of light and shadow into the similar interstice between the central entrance portico vault and its neighbors.

The second shift sets up five bands (between the six iterations of the vault in the east-west direction) of service functions: on the interior space providing for air conditioning ducts, electrical runners, lamps and partition clips, and, on the exterior, between the portico vaults and the first enclosing vault, providing a trench/court for natural light and air to the levels below. At the north and south ends, the bands absorb fire-escape stairs. The whole pattern set up here is repeated in the floor materials: quarter-sawn white oak parquet for the under-vault space, and travertine for the service bands, subdivided in pattern yet again to track the distinction between structural "service" and the hydrodynamic and electrical service.

Interestingly, strict adherence to this banded, intervallic scheme is abandoned in those parts of the lower levels that are already themselves wholly devoted to service: shipping and receiving, workshops, laboratories, and offices. Why? In absolute terms, when servant space is situated in a larger servant space, the difference reasonably dissolves, and with it the need to formalize and iterate the relationship of servant to served. However, even spaces servant to the museum proper, such as restoration laboratories and offices, are themselves servable in turn by "lower" functions, and Kahn maintains not only an unusual amount of design dignity throughout these non-public service areas, but a discipline and graciousness everywhere "below decks," from the security room down to the mechanical rooms, where equipment is immaculately laid out and repeated in rows, and the servant/served distinction is scrupulously followed.[115]

The binary opposition *servant/served,* we begin to see, disseminates, but not wholly in the Derridean fashion, which is to say "horizontally" and non-hierarchically. Rather, it breaks into an articulated, nested, and ranked continuum, a sort of Jacob's ladder. All buildings do this. Kahn merely does it clearly and well. At the Richards Medical Research

Buildings, for example, the service towers dominate, at the Salk Institute the service floors are as large as the served floors but suppressed, visually, to extinction. But it is at the Kimbell that we see Kahn moving toward a rigorous and deconstructive play of literal and phenomenal poché. Neither repressing nor valorizing the servant spaces, he placed them together with the served, as near equals. Between the vaults, they read as marginal, transitional zones of service formally, but nevertheless they work as gallery functionally. Iteratively, subtly (at least in the exhibition area), servant and served are laid into each other with their "natural" hierarchical positioning, daringly, all but erased.[116] (Doug Suisman would go further. From certain views, he observes, the lower sections coalesce to form a low ceiling plane, ". . . and it is this horizontal plane which actually seems to dominate the interior, with the vaults acting merely as vertical interruptions."[117] The hierarchy has been fully, if temporarily, reversed!)

Third, the courtyards. They are three in number, and square. All are placed symmetrically in plan, i.e. centrally, in each wing and, quite sensibly, provide light into the deepest, most interior space.

Now, we have established that Kahn has designated light and lighting as a servant function. Why, then, are the courtyards located in opposition to the intervallic scheme we have been describing? That is, why, if they provide light, are they placed directly in the "served" vault spaces, literally chopping each into sections? Is this Kahn valorizing the servant spaces by preserving their continuity over the continuity of served spaces? Was an optimal courtyard just the wrong shape and size to fit into the scheme of bands?

Indeed, we must conclude that the courtyards are a-sys-

The Kimbell, typical view across vaults.

tematic. They undermine the taxonomy of servant and served, even as they are needed programmatically by the insufficiency of light provided by the overhead luminaire and the incandescent light fixtures. What has Kahn done to show us *his* understanding of the problem?

We notice that the courtyards are very different in size, depth, glazing, and function. One of them, the conservator's court, descends two levels into the building to illuminate the otherwise buried offices and laboratories below. It by-passes the gallery floor, leaving as a trace there four blank, inexplicable, travertine panelled walls and carving out a double-square, rectangular area from the museum.[118] Below, this courtyard is not accessible to the public, but only visible; hence, doubly and triply servant.

The second, so-called fountain courtyard is tiny. Glazed only on two sides and shaded, it contains a fountain and a sculpture of perfect symmetry and maternal femininity that are aligned to inscribe a minor east-west axis in the south

The Kimbell, Conservator's Court looking south, lower level.

The Kimbell, Fountain Court looking east.

wing. The light from this courtyard is soft and intimate. Its solid walls, north and south, in sealing the interrupted vaulted space, would go right to the underside of the vault itself except for the arced window.

The third, "north court" is as large as the second is small, and as present as a courtyard as the first, the conservator's, is absent. It is glazed on four sides completely, right up to the soffit of the vault on the north and south faces. The light it provides is considerable.[119] Tables for the coffee shop are set outdoors. A sculpture of maternality's complement ("L'Air" by Aristide Maillol) occupies the center and establishes a long north-south inner axis to the entire building.

Thus we see Kahn choose, not an iterated element in a changing context, as he does so strictly with the vaults, but the complement of this system: an element that resists its own iteration, that re-defines, re-shapes, re-sizes, and re-renders itself as differently as is feasible while still being a functional "courtyard." The *that* which is iterated and carefully insisted upon is, thus, not a form (even squareness is lost in the perception), but an experience, an idea about light-found-within, about light at the heart of shaded space, an oasis in reverse. In plan too, the three courtyards are situated in a staggered pattern, lest they be seen aligned together and therefore in some hierarchy.

The experience of the building confirms our reading of the plan. First, most visitors to the museum think of the courts as dropped in casually. They are not. Next, so thoroughly has Kahn erased it that most people on the gallery level are simply not aware of the conservator's court, finding its presence on the lower level thus absolutely marvelous and surprising. Last, one may begin to see how the recessed west entry—enclosed on three sides by walls and glazing, and on the fourth by a grove of small trees that closes off the

The Kimbell, Conservator's Court looking north.

view back to the streets and cars as one steps from under them and up into the entrance portico—is a courtyard of sorts too.[120] Upon reflection, one realizes that a rich, hierarchical scheme of internalities and centerings has been instated, one with "horizontal" and "vertical" iterations far deeper than, and counterpointed to, the more conspicuous repetitions of the building.

Fourth in our list of "displacements" is the way in which the vaults are ended against walls. We have already paid some attention to this in our discussion of the play of different curvatures here. All that need be pointed out in addition is that the vaults do not touch exterior east and west walls either, but rather hover just one foot above them along the entire length. Thus the remarkable span of the vault as such is re-marked, and once more a slit of light is allowed in; but now not only to serve with illumination, but to hint of a harsher, brighter outside beyond, the world that has established, in response, this filtered, protected, stone place.

Fifth and most dramatic is the way each vault (except the portico vaults) is split down the middle and opened up for light from the sky. At once radical and obvious, it was a "move" that needed to be covered up immediately, not only because too much light would be allowed in, but because of the destruction and trivialization of the vault form that would have resulted. Kahn's intention was to re-create the, *a*, sky: a heavenly vault. The valorization here is palpable. For the new, iterated sky to be "sky," however, a smooth and mysteriously originated light must be emitted from it. With the suspended, perforated metal reflector (a significant invention in its own right) both the erasure of the slot and the redistribution of light is effected. The sky is denied, admitted, reversed, and reinstated; the breach remains but is healed.

A problematic yet ultimately confirmatory reading of the vault as sky is provided by the well-known photograph of Louis Kahn standing cross-legged at the bottom of the auditorium (page 39 of *Light Is the Theme*). A sliver of sunlight glimmers across the travertine beside him, like a beam from heaven. Now, the picture was taken during construction, before the necessary darkening baffles were put into the skylight, which is interesting enough, but in any case, no direct sunlight is supposed to be able to penetrate the reflector in the first place. Kahn seizes the ephemeral, the wrong, the accidental, the incomplete . . . as the essence, and signs the reading of "unsolicited blessing," or grace, with his personal presence.[121] In another transformation, another displacement of the figure, on page 13 of the same book, a transitory crescent of sunlight falling upon the entry portico floor is effectively captioned by the accompanying text as a "slice of the sun." The words are Kahn's, quoting an unnamed poet, but are grafted from another context by the compiler of the book, Nell Johnson. This picture of an marginal event—one that can happen only in one location in the building, and at certain moments of the year and day, moments themselves insignificant—is thus now cast as a *ver-*

The Kimbell, Louis Kahn in the auditorium during construction.

The Kimbell, "slice of sun" on entry porch.

ification of Kahn's entire system of ideas, and through an appropriated trope to boot.[122]

Another image that Kahn used to describe the vaults and the kind of light he saw from them was that of "a moth, spreading its wings."[123] This image captures ambiguously both the vault and the reflector, their silver lightness tying it obliquely to both the idea of flight and therefore air and sky, the base or original metaphor.

At the more formal level: What of the esoteric curvature and fixing of the reflectors? Their curves are neither elliptical nor cycloidal but parabolic; they are doubled and creased where the vaults are smoothest and most whole, inverted and hung where the vaults are "erect," and supported as though tracing a motion $90°$ out of phase. Their lightness is of a different sort from the vaults, their sheer size surprising and unapologized for. They are both intrusions and foils, marginal and central—servant elements that dominate and efface themselves at once.

The contradictions, the multiplicity of (mis)readings, are left standing. With regard to the reflector, in fact, they are insisted upon in just the way I mentioned in my discussion of iterability. For the reflector is a constant feature of a constant feature, the interior vault, and it appears in areas dark enough to require it direly as well as in areas—next to the north court for example—where its effect is bleached out and its function is locally redundant. If I might quote myself from an earlier page: "Notice, however, that for the (once-unique) configuration to be seen as *meaningful* it cannot seem automatic or reflexive, a given given the situation, nor too molded by its context. Thus the importance of subtle *misuse* in thematizing a form or figure. By duplicating and displacing it against a heterogeneous background, by under-adapting it to the contexts of its re-appearances, by hinting at—flirting with—unnaturalness and nonfunctionality, it becomes, first, an 'it,' a 'figure' at all, and then the carrier of unspecified significance."[124]

Sixth, and subtle to the point of invisibility, is how conditioned air is admitted to the gallery spaces. Between the vaults, in the seven-foot band, run the air supply ducts, given ample room and announced, yet absorbed silently into the whole formal scheme. The soffit is fabricated from anodized aluminum panels (for accessibility as well as to distinguish its servant function) and is dropped below the bottom of the vault spring line to create a horizontal slot immediately beneath the vault iterating the slot along the outside. From this fissure, this incomplete closing, the air flows. Air return is handled through long floor ducts, again, strictly within the servant zone.

The seventh item of our list is fairly self-explanatory. The way water is *introduced* into a pool is always a problem for an architect sensitive to the issue of "naturalness" (as is the opposite problem of where the water is to go). We know that technically there is no difficulty here. We all accept the reality of pumps and sumps in this modern day as well as the fact that ornamental water is (responsibly) re-circulated; but a good designer feels duty-bound to embrace, or at least be unambiguous about, either a naturalistic or artificial ideal as informing his efforts. In the first case one may seek to "mime" a geyser or a rock cleft, seepage from a bank, or a stream of inflow from afar; in the second, anything amazing will do, although repeating an example from architectural history (let us say, the fountains at Trevi or Tivoli) is a safe bet. Gargoyles and pseudo-scuppers are also an option, blending in more naturalistic indications of rainwater or seepage. And so on. At the Kimbell, Kahn suppresses the whole issue in its literal, technical aspects, and we find only a hint of the "seepage/cleft" natural archetype in the slot that runs fully along the outer portico floor and past the benches. We see the water beginning its slide from

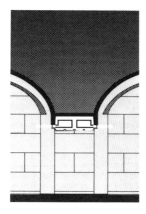

The Kimbell, diagrammatic section through
air conditioning service zone.

under the floor, through an opening not unlike the air conditioning inlets inside, and into the open pool.

The eighth caesura is one that deserves a treatment outside this subsection. Nevertheless, I will treat it here, and return to it in another context.

Clearly, the double stair from the lower east entrance lobby to the upper museum is located, like all of the stairs, in a servant zone. In mimesis of the natural archetype, the stair form is treated as a crack or crevice, perhaps a collapse or rockfall, and one *ascends* to light and view rather than descends to them, as is proper. This gives the stairs a privileged direction. But notice this: the operative, essential, and valorized floor of the Kimbell is the upper one. Here are the vaults, the art, the coffee shop and bookstore, the light, the view to the park, and the best entrance to the building. The Kimbell wishes to be a one-story building, a plane, a rippled field of space not unlike the treed one nearby. Kahn wishes to deny, if not the very existence of the lower floor, then its connection to the upper. And this he achieves (a) by designating the stairs between as "servant," (b) by making them modest in size, and, most importantly, (c) by aligning them so that, although they are centrally located, they are effectively invisible from the upper level. The solid travertine-faced balustrade and the proximity of the upper landings to a blank wall ensure that the presence of the shape and possibility of descent is suppressed, and that the entire lower level does not communicate visually with the upper. We also recall how the conservator's court eschews the opportunity

The Kimbell, slit of originating water.

for vertical visual connection, and how, outdoors, the entire lower level is denied travertine finish, appearing as a mere concrete platform for the upper.

(The correct entrance, the one Kahn so carefully orchestrated from west, north, and south, is the upper one. The lower is treated as a service zone. Kahn was ambivalent about our automobile society, at times praising the car for its freedom and animal grace, at others striving to remove people from them as soon as possible and set them on their feet. What he did not manage at the Kimbell was to provide for, or designate, parking in such a way that the valorized entry was easiest. Like most architects, he underestimated, or was unwilling to accept, how committed Americans are to their cars and to the convenience of parking them as close as physically possible to their destinations.[125])

Last is the way Kahn handles joints between different materials. Everywhere it is the same: the joint is recessed. The building valorizes the difficult-to-achieve flushness of planes; all "muscularity," all formal athleticism or additive, assemblative complexity other than the prime statement of the vaults, is suppressed. What remains is delineation of dif-

The Kimbell, lobby and bookstore.

The Kimbell, stair at lower level.

ferences within the plane, and this without covering or re-indicating them, without relief or molding.

The overall effect is and is not salutary. With flushness, simple repetition, and soft colors everywhere, Kahn creates a place of considerable serenity and control for the viewing of art. But what happens all too often is that actual paintings, especially older ones, can seem grotesquely three-dimensional and physical. Often dark in tone, their thick frames hang away from the travertine walls and flush wood panels, casting shadows from the incandescent fixtures. The Kimbell in fact is somewhat better suited to presenting tapestries, small sculptures, and items that can be shown in cases.[126]

6. THE WEST ENTRY

I have discussed the west entry a number of times already in different contexts. I would ask the reader to bear them in mind as I pose the question:What is a "portico"?

A portico is a covered, often colonnaded ambulatory, near the entrance of a (usually classical) building, says Webster's. And just in case "portico" is merely a graceful Italianate locution for a porch, we find a "porch" defined as a covered entrance to a building, usually with a separate roof, and often large enough for seating and walking. The Kimbell's three westernmost vaults seem to fit both definitions.

But we notice immediately that their function at the Kimbell is reinterpreted if not compromised by their radical truncation and discontinuity. Their status as porches (which is how Kahn referred to them, "portico" appearing on the drawings) is challenged. Because they are discontinuous, it is not possible, for example, to move from portico to portico without getting wet if it is raining, nor to get into a wait-

The Kimbell, artificial lighting of paintings.

ing car anywhere. One cannot arrive at them frontally with ease, so remote are they from the street. Further, the two side vaults are for walking along, not across, just as the center one is for walking across, not along.

"Who cares?" one might say. "It never rains in Forth Worth; intense heat and dryness is the dominant problem, and shade (and water) and a walk-across park is what is provided." Nevertheless, Kahn seems conscious of the critique he has wrought upon the Classical model that would provide true porticos *and* the Modernist, form-follows-function model that would provide the facility in some new way. The porches are unnecessary and marginal: offerings to a non-existent street.[127] After telling us that "[b]ecause of the porches, how the building is made is completely clear before you go into it," and thus casting them as prologomenical, as *overture* (somewhat inaccurately, since the sectional character of the entire building is clearly shown from north or south approach, and since the porch vaults are neither interrupted nor possess the all-important top-lighting that the interior ones do, and thus do *not* make clear how the rest of the vaults are made), he goes on to say:

It is the same realization behind Renaissance buildings which gave the arcade to the street, though the buildings themselves did not need the arcade for their own purposes. So the porch sits there, made as the interior is made, without any obligation of paintings on its walls [we will later have reason to remark about this "obligation"], a realization of what is architecture. When you look at the building and the porch, it is an offering. You know it wasn't programmed; it is something that emerged.[128]

"You know what is so wonderful about these porches?" he then asks, rhetorically. "They're so unnecessary."[129]

Here we see illustrated a perfect example of a *parergonal* figure, perhaps more perfect than a typical "Renaissance arcade," which really was quite integral to the structure, function, and visual composition of the building in an urban setting. Here, that which is professedly supplemental ends up not only representing and prefacing the whole at its margins, but standing as the quintessential statement of the architect's intention throughout. Relative to such a preface, the rest of the "text" is posed as a corruption, a yielding to competing themes and obligations.

With two more closed vaults (or one fewer) Kahn could have run three open portico vaults continuously across the west facade.[130] But he did not. The all-important central entry portico is displaced two modules "back," to the east, leaving a void that must be crossed. This kind of subtraction or withdrawal from the centerline, this introduction of emptiness not as a kind of shaped space in the classical mode but as an ache, a lack, Kahn thought of as the creation of Silence: a Hegelian clearing for the arrival of the ineffable. Sentries to this space, the vaults themselves seem to be holding their breath.[131] This created void at the Kimbell is not empty but filled; however, not as at the Salk Institute (where Luis Barragan had persuaded Kahn not to plant trees). It is filled in a most interesting way: fifty-two small yaupon holly trees line up, close, on a square grid, the two aisles on either side of the all-but-erased east-west axis aligning perfectly with the two glass doors to the museum. Here the slender yaupons seem to populate the space with evocations of gathering and orderly waiting to enter.[132]

More: an elegant set of categorical oppositions is set up between the character of this space and the shifted portico vault spaces that make it possible, indeed necessary. To wit: the vaults are high and light and empty, the grove of trees low and dark and settled; the vaults are directional, graceful, and controlled, the grove is diffusing, gnarled, and, though aligned, natural. The scale of the vaults is heroic and their strength uncanny, the grove is human, even humble, and the individual trees are lashed and wired to support their delicate foliage. The porticos show people off (one looks wonderful and singular in the clear, high space with slanted sunshine) while the grove absorbs people, making of them shadows, flitting between trunks, percolating through. The vaults place hardness above and below us with steel-smooth

The Kimbell, looking south among the yaupons.

and exposed-aggregate concrete respectively; the grove places softness above and below us: the low leaves over, the gravel crunching closely underfoot. One can pick up on the whole system of oppositions from any one of them individually. They seem to lead to and cause each other, to reverberate; to be, in some sense, the *same* opposition proliferated and extended. Derrida would say: disseminated.

And one might dream of this retreated, impeding, yet honorific entry space with its solemn grove and gravel as evocative of death and transition: a lowness and fading of crisp light and of elevation before re-emergence into a softer light.[133]

One, more "practical," reading. In Chinese geomancy, long hallways of space are to be avoided. When they cannot be avoided, a "fix" is supplied; namely, one hangs a wind-chime or chandelier in the hall, best near the center of its length. The chandelier diffuses, de-fuses, the force and velocity of *ch'i*, but without blocking it entirely and thus causing both disfunction and the bad feeling of stoppage. At the Kimbell, the two, aligned portico vaults, viewed from either end and creating a spatial channel 300 feet long, would, without the low grove of trees, generate enormous *ch'i*. (Three aligned vaults would have generated an even stronger force.) The grove is thus a critical in(ter)vention: a wind chime, a softener, a disperser, of spatial velocity in the north-south direction, as much as a filter for *ch'i* from the slope to the west we discussed earlier.

Passing from the grove on into the building, one steps up to and under the central portico, barely clearing one's head of the low branches. This portico vault is darker, more interior; and one's attention is now caught by the lovely way that direct and reflected light falls at its ends, on the floor, and

The Kimbell, west entry porticos, diagram of ch'i *"dispersed" by yaupons.*

on the walls of the vaults between which it rests. This lighting—this "spending" of Light, as Kahn would put it—is a unique condition, and occurs nowhere else. The condition is not contrived, however. Rather, it emerges in the best way: naturally, epiphenomenally, as a result of a system of making, of forces and rules whose "interest" lies elsewhere, with their own playing out.

Turning around here, about to enter the building (or just emerging from it and looking ahead) the grove of yaupons now precisely obscures Camp Bowie Boulevard, Will Rogers West, and Lancaster Ave. One is already *in.* I remarked upon

The Kimbell, west entry, under yaupons looking east.

The Kimbell, west entry portico looking north.

The Kimbell, west entry portico looking west.

this earlier. Another effect is apparent, however, from this portico and from the interior lobby looking out: the grove trees, because they are small, slender, closely spaced, and *close by*, blend in dimensionally with the larger, older, more distantly spaced and distant trees of the park. In a reversal of "forced perspective," and without obvious linear clues, the grove at hand is absorbed into the more distant park. Conversely, rather than feeling an encroachment by an un-adjusted, full-scale landscape upon the building (which is without—we should remember—any high and forceful en-try form), we feel instead the moderation, the slowing down, the collecting, taming, and regularizing of outdoor energies.

And so, as we pay close attention to the causes of our expe-rience, we can "read" the west entry as a flux of motions and contrasts, real and potential, visual and kinesthetic. Self-de-constructively, as it were, what is artificial (the vault) is in-vited to show its natural strength, and what is natural (wa-ter, trees) to obey an artificial plan. Entry is valorized, but without elevation, and thus without pushing all else in its path away or breaking the system of traces. Certain differ-ences are crisply insisted upon: others are melded and dis-solved only to be inscribed again elsewhere, deferred.

Could any or all of these deconstructive "plays" have been achieved some other way, by some other arrangement of forms, spaces, and details? Clearly, not exactly. But I think that in kind and in general the answer must be "yes," even as we admire Kahn's mastery here. The manifestations of Ar-chitecture are not to be limited. But over and above these contrasts, structures, and movements (which, as the reader will recall, I gave the role of forming only the *armature* of meaning rather than its living import, which are all but void

The Kimbell, longitudinal section showing control of view
by yaupons.

of meaning in themselves, and which, besides, many less-good buildings share in kind) both the vaults and the grove at the west side of the Kimbell are unique and specific in their mimetic action. Each re-produces figurations of a natural or early urban environment and, deeper, each appeals directly to certain stances, scenes, and situations of our most physical/biological selves. I will leave the reader to meditate further upon the specifics of such scenes. For describe them as I might, the very procedure of meditation—if the reader might look at the building again—is wherein meaning is freshly released. Evocations continue, overlap, and fade into one another; none seem to be final. And perhaps I have described too many already.

7. THE LIBRARY

Where is the library? It does not appear often in published plans; it certainly does not appear at all in the building to any casual visitor. Indeed, the library is hidden as though by sleight of hand behind the flush cabinetry of the bookshop and in an upper (third) level right under the central vault. The two doors in the cabinetry are barely noticeable, literally camouflaged.

The space behind is intimate, comfortable, and unremarkable. The upper level is distinctly compressed under the vault, especially since there are a multitude of (retrofitted) boxy, fluorescent lighting fixtures hanging below the reflector. (The "pressure" is relieved, however, by the glazed ends and the floor level light admitted along the length of the vault, the iterated slot now re-cast as a window.) On the outside no indication is given of this unique function and use of the vault system.

One hardly knows what to make of this. Did Kahn simply run out of space? Is all the concealment a result of some embarrassment that this servant function—the library—finds itself in a served zone on the main level? The library may be private in the sense of not being casually visitable by the public, but is this not carrying things too far?

Adopting a Derridean (if not Freudian) frame of mind, it all begins to make sense, though much of what follows is conjecture on my part quite directly.

Louis Kahn was Jewish. That is to say, from the perspective of modern non-Jews in Western democracies, he was a member of that ephemeral, (today) loosely connected society called, and calling itself, "the People of the Book." The book referred to here, of course, is the Old Testament of the Bible. But more than two thousand years of hermetic devotion to this book's text has made the Jewish people, especially through the last three or four hundred years, the "people of all books"—or, less vaingloriously, simply a bookish people. The Jewish value system places education, literacy, expres-

The Kimbell, bookstore.

The Kimbell, closet cabinetry and door to library.

The Kimbell, library interior.

sion, and discovery *through the written word* above almost all other values save obedience to the Ten Commandments.[134]

Historically, to a Jew as to a Moslem, all representational visual art risks idolatry. Of course, when there *was* only representational painting and sculpture this position was more reasonable to take, especially in view of the pietistic, patronistic, and impositional symbolic functions Western art has performed over the major part of its history. Materiality, fine craftsmanship, embellishment of texts and garments, the placement of things just so . . . these private, marginal, nonpersonal and largely non-representational modes of visual artistic production were all that were encouraged in Jewish aesthetic culture. Until the advent of modern art, abstraction, and a larger, more egalitarian art world in this century, poring over the Book, poring over books, debating, telling stories, pursuing mathematics, law, medicine or music, *writing* . . . these were the more legitimate undertakings for a young Jew. Such was the ideological home environment in which Kahn (and, perhaps not incidentally here, Derrida and Eisenman) grew up.[135]

Now, in all this, architecture plays an ambiguous role. Though visual and tactile, it is not obviously representational, even historically, and with the great temple builders of the Bible as exemplars, only lack of connection to power, capital, and, in many places, the right to own land, had kept Jews from entering the profession. Akin to geometry and music, architecture is a pre- or non-verbal writing of sorts, closer to *arche-writing,* if we follow Derrida's reasoning,[136] than to any real writing. The possibility of idolatry, which depends on pictorial or conventional reference, seems remote, especially in the Modernist idiom. For Kahn, at any rate—a bookish man, a raconteur, a pianist, and a violinist—architecture clearly presented a way of spiritual service somehow deeper, more real, and more glorious than any other.

And yet here he was, being asked (for the first time)[137] to create a museum of mostly historical art: a place of paintings, artifacts, small sculptures, treasures, and, quite literally, idols.

His response was this: to withdraw the Book from view, place thresholds around it, and elevate it to sacredness at the same time. In seclusion, study gains value; in remoteness, the Word lives undisturbed. Thus we find the library hidden in the midst of commerce, as though the ark of the covenant were being trundled through a marketplace in a covered wagon. (Now the vaults are repetitions of the ark, the wagon, canvas covers billowing.) Placed most centrally, and placed potentially most visibly of all the functional volumes in the building—that is, right at the east entrance, directly over the west one and on axis—the library is a region yet most inaccessible, dissimulated, and camouflaged, erased from consciousness by the bland sweep of cabinet wood. The museum-goer leafs through picture books and recipe books at the bookstore untroubled. Money changes hands. Or he wanders past in search of something remarkable in this light-as-air cave. (Now the vaults appear as stone niches for idols, especially at their ends, not built but carved; or as sarcophagi laid side by side. . . .) Yet, by all accounts, the Kimbell Art Museum is a functional success as a place for the presentation of art objects for those to whom art objects are the figure, the "point."

Kahn, the Modernist, the architect, the man of the world, would never have told us this—that his building tells us. He had only noble things to say about art, which he saw, at its best, as an expression by one man of the commonness that exists between men. "A work of art is an offering to Art,"[138] he said; but he had said the same of architecture many times. His discussions of art went quickly to his favorite themes of Beauty, Order, Desire, Light, and so on; and one begins to realize that Kahn, though he admired Picasso, Cezanne, Rembrandt, and the rest, had remarkably little specific to say about painting, sculpture, photography, film, or any of the arts but architecture. If anything, he had given more thought to science, philosophy, and fairy tales: "I believe in the fairy tale," he once declared. "I believe in the wish of the fairy tale as the beginning of science. I'd much rather write cryptic things, and then do something."[139] Kahn's buildings were also his writing, however. For him, for us, they have always been "cryptic things." And none is more cryptic than the Kimbell.

D. IN CONCLUSION

In both Kahn and Derrida we see the struggle with logo-centrism, that predilection from our metaphysical heritage to place the Truth in the Word. Though Kahn, in Neopla-tonic fashion, would have his signifiers end their course, or have their origin, in Order or Silence, and Derrida would have his be grounded in *différance*, which is to say, not be "grounded" at all, they both share the intuition that presence itself devolves not upon some locatable place and time, but upon some originary trace whose shape is unindicatable.

> *Silence to Light*
> *Light to Silence*
> *The threshold of their crossing*
> *is the Singularity* . . .

writes Kahn.[140] One reads here the attempt to locate mean-ing in a movement situated impossibly near by and far away, at a moment infinitely diaphanous.

Derrida and Kahn share also what perhaps is the fate of all philosophers and poets who circumnavigate the margins of language: the ring of interlinked, almost interchangeable key-words—for Kahn: Light, Order, Form, Design, Desire, Expression, capitalized always to signify their Platonic dig-nity; for Derrida: *différance*, the *arche*-trace, writing, *brisure*, alterity, and many others worked almost unan-nounced into the thickness of his texts—around which their readers follow them in what amounts to faith.

Of the same situation Derrida's vision is heroically tragic, Kahn's more simply heroic. Where Derrida sees the "know-able" world as nothing but the active proliferation of traces, and sees all that is witnessable in its presence as only a half, a remainder from some global retraction, self-splitting, or Fall still permeating every crack and every word, Kahn posits a unknowable Beginning that has in it already the desire for presence, for joy in being, for movement and breaking through the threshold from Silence to Light, "the giver of all presences." The writer/philosopher can do no more than supplement indefinitely what has been written and thought without beginning, but the artist/architect's calling is to turn his intuition of ultimates toward the bringing forth and cre-ation anew of such presences as bear the mark of authentic origin. For Derrida's writer/philosopher there can be only a

Sisyphean carrying-on, with no closer approach to Truth or Being possible; for Kahn's architect, every building is an "offering to Architecture," which, though itself undoubtedly inadequate, may be so by degrees.

Derrida would find Kahn's ideas—and one must remember here that Kahn was not a professional philosopher —soaked in the "metaphysics of presence," which it is his aim to question. But, let us note, if for Kahn light was the maker of presences, it could not operate without material and without shadow (words he would occasionally capitalize). "Material is spent light" was one of Kahn's favorite dicta. This poetically stated but rather practical observation (if by "practical" we mean: subject to the discipline of physical feasibility, even if as only an image) shows us a man not unaware of how presences become present: through a kind of death, a giving over to absence, in movement. The realms of Silence, Form, and Order Kahn called "immeasurable," and he was unable and unwilling to smash through to their essence with logistical, analytical tools. He knew where to leave off. A man as inarticulate with the written form as Derrida is articulate, perhaps Kahn felt he could not go any farther with words. Perhaps he knew—wanted—his buildings to make the final sortie, and of the kind that only buildings can make.[141]

I think we find Derrida in a less fortunate position. Derrida has ploughed up the certain earth of *logos*, and has not allowed himself to see that in his very ploughing, in the tools he has most excellently fashioned, and in the ancient seeds his metaphors broadcast again, lies the real story. Or perhaps he has.

In all, when we put Kahn and Derrida together as I have attempted to do, two summary observations emerge that describe them in complementary terms. On the one hand we have Derrida, whose writing is shot through with natural, spatial, architectonic, and human-life metaphors along whose contours, paradoxically and self-deconstructively, entire arguments move—arguments denying depth, natural foundations, and/or transcendence to signified/signifier relationships—and yet from whose emotion-laden, originary substance he taps meaning without rest. On the other hand we have Louis Kahn, a man who spoke passionately of nature and human nature, essences and inexpressibles, presences and origins, and of the shape that architecture gives to these, and who yet, at his finest hour, made a building that ingeniously skirted establishing any of them by declaration and created instead, and with effectiveness for his purpose, a "text" so full of the traces of *différance*, so full of the equalizations, contradictions, openness to grafts, and infinitely subtle readings we are helped to see with the theory of Deconstruction, that one has to wonder at the logic of it all. To put it very roughly: Derrida speaks of differences but writes with essences, Louis Kahn spoke of essences, but built with differences.

The task of comparing all Kahn's written and spoken work to Derrida's is one that would be lengthy indeed, as would be a deconstruction of Kahn's philosophy and built work (which, of course, is not the same thing). Rather, let us return to one of the simpler and, we might now feel, less important questions we began with: Is the Kimbell Art Museum a (proto)Deconstructivist work of architecture, one that might have appeared in Johnson and Wigley's MoMA catalog had it been built fifteen years later?

The answer has to be no. This, even though formally —stylistically—it is made of many, long, narrow parts, shifted apart with many slits and slots, it is non-hierarchical, it stretches the usual limits of structural engineering, it is boldly modern and yet not streamlined or technoid, it creates a field of action and incident without over-specification, it is critical of its circumstances, and it is and looks construc*ted*. We say no because the Kimbell means something other than its own devices and it appeals to something other than attention to its subversions. The Kimbell is controlled rather than anarchic in geometry and materiality, and bears little resemblance to Russian Constructivism. Each dislocation functions not to disrupt but to connect. It illustrates no Deconstructionist text, and refrains also from amoral play with emblems and random structures.

And yet the Kimbell may be taken as what we would *want* to mean by Deconstruction in architecture; as somehow a truer exemplar for a future architecture that has learned from, rather than still illustrates, the philosophy of Deconstruction. Let us examine this proposition more closely.

The Kimbell is no ordinarily excellent building (if such can be said!): few buildings evidence so gracefully and intentionally traces from all the depths, all levels, from geometrical eternals through the evolved and evolving natural and so-

cial patterns, to evanescent moments of individual consciousness. Nevertheless it is true that many (but not all) excellent buildings *can* be deconstructed critically and philo-
sophically to good effect along lines that may or may not look
like mine. In the next few years, I surmise, we are likely to see
seminal works in the oeuvre of Aalto, Le Corbusier, Wright,
and Mies van der Rohe interpreted through Deconstruction.[142] After all, as the literary critic J. Hillis Miller says:

*Great works of literature [architecture] are likely to be
ahead of their critics. They are there already. They have an-
ticipated explicitly any deconstruction the critic can
achieve. A critic may hope, with great effort, and with the
indispensable help of the authors [architects] themselves, to
raise himself to the level of literary [architectural] sophis-
tication where . . . [Praxiteles, Michelangelo, Palladio,
Wren, Le Corbusier, Kahn, or even Venturi] . . . are already.
They are there already, however, necessarily in such a way
that their works are open to mystified readings.[143]*

"The critic's task," Culler elaborates (citing Miller further), is
"to identify an act of deconstruction which has always already, and in each case differently, been performed by the
text [building] itself." One focuses on meanings and operations "thematized in the text [building] itself in the form of
metalinguistic [meta-architectural] statements" which wait
there, in tense coexistence, for acts of identification which
will bring them out.[144]

And an architect's task, presumably, is to provide the
material.

But I would stop short of saying that "deconstructibility"
is either a prerequisite or desideratum for great architecture,
the way Miller seems to imply is the case for great literature.
The "greatness" of the Kimbell should not be considered
that which makes it especially deconstructable ipso facto.
Rather, it is that the Kimbell—and all of Kahn's later work—
was designed with ideas that bear peculiar affinities, if often
obversely, to the ideas of Deconstruction, affinities this essay has tried to demonstrate. Certainly, as I have remarked
before, the very metaphysical ambition of his work marks it
as (one hates to use the word) a "target" for Deconstruction
as well as the site for its production, as it were. Reconciling
Kahn's elusive verbal discourse with his direct building style
only adds to the mystification. That indeed Kahn's buildings

can profitably be "read" in terms of that elusive discourse *or not*—that is, that his buildings are traces of his thought that contain, state, reiterate, and go beyond his verbally accessible ideas on their *own* as well as function smoothly and delight the layman—is a considerable achievement, especially in view of the extreme economy of his means and his successful avoidance of self-conscious "textuality" in the built object.

Albeit in proto-form then, the Kimbell fairly might represent what one would *want* to mean by Deconstruction as a method of design and criticism in architecture, as I have said. If so, architects, architectural critics, theorists, and teachers might begin to see how the whole post-structuralist, Deconstructivist movement in architecture might mature, both holding on to and enlivening—because genuinely, deeply, intellectually challenging—architecture's received truths and metaphysical claims. Certainly much current Deconstructivist work with its empty Derridean rhetoric, depthless "superpositions," formulaic "disjunctions," and its alternately fetishized or ignored materiality, would, or could, recede. Lyotard, Baudrillard, Foucault, Deleuze, et al.—post-structuralist thinkers often indiscriminately lumped together with Derrida—may be right in identifying disorientation, fragmentation, and inauthenticity as characterizing our "post-industrial" culture, just as Marshall McLuhan was right twenty years ago about the impact of media and simultaneity on modern life. But it is another step to embrace these conditions by illustrating them quite so literally, or at all, in that medium—architecture—which is most old, most deep, and most necessary to our orientation. Louis Kahn at the Kimbell shows us one way both to think *with* architecture today, and to "write" those thoughts down *in* architecture, this without turning a building into a clever scribble about the futility of meaning. Maintaining connection with man's deepest expectations of buildings, he shows us too, does not condemn us to repeating the valorized forms of any recent past, but rather opens up an investigation of architecture's means and meaning that we have not yet begun in earnest. Understanding Derrida's Deconstruction will be essential to this new and unprecedentedly detailed undertaking.

As for Jacques Derrida and his understanding of himself in relation to architecture, we read from an interview in 1987, some twenty years after *Writing and Difference,* this:

I have the feeling my architectural model must be read in my text. So Glas *or* La Carte Postale *is an organization of space.* Glas, *for instance is not only a book on the theme of the column in Hegel. It is in itself an architecture, a natural artifact. . . . I have the feeling that my repressed desire for music and architecture comes back through my writing, and is what interests me in writing . . .*

I am unable to draw out of my text an architectural model. But if there is one, well, read the text.

Inhabit the text, if you can.[145]

In deconstructing the Kimbell, if this I have done, I have attempted to show how the questions raised by Deconstruction are both askable and answerable in that text finally without words, and that defining condition of "inhabitation," architecture itself.

Diagrammatic series showing excisions from "infinite field" and the evolving system of separations and betweens.

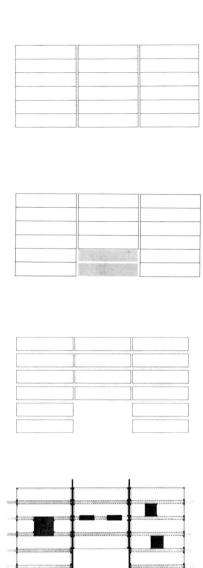

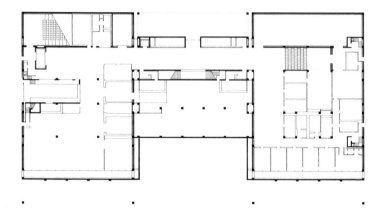

The Kimbell, lower floor plan.

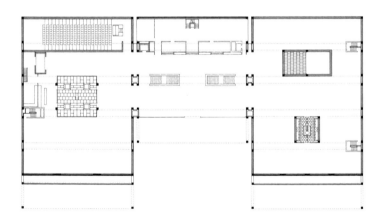

The Kimbell, upper floor plan.

1. This accompanying the Deconstructivist Architecture show at the Museum of Modern Art, Summer 1988. (New York: NY Graphic Soc., 1988).

2. Vol. 58: 3/4; St Martin's.

3. See the more recent Andreas Papadakis, Catherine Cooke, and Andrew Benjamin, eds., *Deconstruction: The Omnibus Volume* (New York: Rizzoli, 1989) and *Reconstruction Deconstruction, Architectural Design* 59 (1989).

See also the earlier *AA Files* (London: The Architecture Association), especially vols. 13, 14 (1986, 1987); *The Culture of Fragments,* in Columbia's *Precis* 6 (Spring 1987); Yale's *Perspecta* 23 (1988); MIT's *Assemblage* 7 (1988); and U. Texas Center for the Study of American Architecture's *Center: A Journal for American Architecture* 4 (1988), especially Robert Mugerauer, "Derrida and Beyond," 66-75.

Of course, individuals such as Peter Eisenman, Bernard Tschumi, and Daniel Liebeskind have been promulgating Deconstruction for some time.

4. For an intelligent example see Philip H. Bess, "Deconstruction: A Brief Critique of a Critical Theory," *Inland Architect* (Jan/Feb 1988).

5. The movement's leaders, of course, at first wished to shrug off the label as either meaningless or not applicable to them. But then, they always do. For many years, not a single Postmodernist (except perhaps Robert Stern) ever called himself a "Postmodernist."

As for Deconstructivism's promoters, Philip Johnson (in *Deconstructivist Architecture*) avers that "no matter how delicious it would be to declare a new style, Deconstructivism is not a new style," while Mark Wigley reportedly ended the symposium that accompanied the MoMA show "by noting that they had at least achieved one of [its] purposes, 'to kill the word off'" (Gastil, see below). Similarly, at Tigerman's ACSA Chicago Forum on Architectural Issues in October 1988, talk was that "Deconstructivism" had to go, to be replaced by the vaguer and larger "Post-structuralism." Why all the disingenuousness, the deferral?

As reported with some delight by Raymond Gastil in a *Design Book Review* article [Fall 1988: 66], itself a disparaging "what's-all-the-fuss-about?-this-is-socially-irrelevant" re-

view of the book, the show, and the symposium, set in an issue of *DBR* paradoxically laced with new, Deconstruction-
style criticism) Wigley's behavior is normal for the circumstances: attempting to be both responsible and not
responsible for the good or harm that might come from students and architects in the sticks making their own sense of,
and then rallying around, a new "ism." As it stands, "Deconstructivism" is the word—the Word—emblazoned on
MoMA's orange-colored catalog/book, and this name is what
has entered the body of architectural ideology, irrevocably,
for however short a time.

6. Charles Jencks, "Deconstruction: The Pleasures of Absence," *Architectural Design* 58: 3/4 (1988). Jencks does
suggest that Peter Eisenman is the only true Deconstructionist.

7. Derrida himself was reportedly both amused by, and ap-
palled at, the new "remote and untouchable architecture"
that has arisen paying allegiance to his ideas: "too bizarre,
too foreign, too *étrange.*" (Reported in John Taylor, "Mr. In-
Between," *New York* 21:41 (October 17, 1988): 51. But this
is of little importance.

8. Two answers to our questions (a) and (b) have already
been published: one from Mark Wigley in his essay in *Deconstructivist Architecture* and one from Michael Sorkin in
an article in *The Village Voice:* "Decon Job" (July 5, 1988).
    Wigley, understandably, says, yes, there is a new move-
ment here (sort of); but, no, there is no strong connection
to Derrida's theory of Deconstruction (not really). Sorkin
says a resounding *no* to both questions: no, Deconstructivism does not accurately encompass or describe the di-
verse work and intentions of the architects in the MoMA
show, and, no, Deconstructivism in architecture has little to
do with Deconstruction in literature and philosophy.
    It must be said that Wigley's denial of the connection to
Derrida's Deconstruction is fragile, if not disingenuous. His
own essay is redolent with Derridaisms—even as he dis-
claims the French connection in the works he discusses.
Writing in English, his home tongue, but affecting the locutions of overly literal translations of academic French, he attempts but fails to explain why clashing, splintered forms
and other varieties of disjunctive geometry (which are just

about all Zaha Hadid and Frank Gehry have in common) are anything more than just a new stylistic twist on things, or why these formal moves constitute a significant cultural critique of the foundations and limits of architecture in any way parallel to the way Derrida's "moves" constitute a critique of the foundations and limits of language. Sorkin goes into this and more, giving us, as he always does, a sharp view of the socio-political dimension of style and fame-mongering in the architectural subculture.

All this matters to the extent that we worry whether Deconstructivism is *just* a style, a "look," a transitory fashion, or whether there is more to it, more behind it, to sustain continued invention and inquiry beyond the heralded "look." There need not be, really. For style and stylistic evolution in art, cinema, publishing, music, architecture run on their own crazy energy and shallow logic, and no one involved need understand deeply or care what is going on for the enterprise to flourish. Indeed, *understanding* is all too often a conservative pressure, a spoil-sportism in a field where relatively value-free sportingness is the very lifeblood of invention and exploration. The serious business of class warfare and economic strategy that *style* covers over is suppressed or dealt with ironically by its creative participants—necessarily. I will leave the reader to judge, having read through this essay, whether my attempts to operate with understanding support stylistic conservatism or not.

9. For example: Christopher Norris, *Derrida* (Cambridge, MA: Harvard UP, 1987); Richard Harland, *Superstructuralism* (New York: Methuen, 1987); Howard Felperin, *Beyond Deconstruction* (New York: Oxford UP, 1985); Philip Rice and Patricia Waugh, eds., *Modern Literary Theory* (New York: Hodder Stoughton, 1989); Frank Lentricchia, *After the New Criticism* (Chicago: Chicago UP, 1980). For an account that leads to considerations for teaching and the arts, see Gregory Ulmer, *Applied Grammatology* (Baltimore: Johns Hopkins UP, 1985). For a lighter look at the whole scene, see Richard A. Shweder, "In Paris—Miniskirts of the Mind," *The New York Times Book Review* (Jan 8, 1989): 1.

10. How Derrida *reverses* this direction of influence, that is, how Derrida's interest in the phenomena of philosophical discourse is guided by an intuition for architectural—or per-

haps I should say "architectonic"—phenomena, is something I hope to have shown plausibly by the end of the essay.

11. For watching the English language in full Deconstructionist flower in its own right—i.e., not in translation from the French, nor in tortured explanation—see Geoffrey Hartman's *Easy Pieces* (New York: Columbia UP, 1985).

12. Some believe that Derrida's intentions are nihilistic; nihilistic in the sense that, in so relentlessly questioning the metaphysics of presence and absence (which is to say, all of Western metaphysics), he is presenting as an alternative, as a set of "values," chaos, ignorance, and endless fruitless discourse. I think not. Let us turn this over a little in our minds.

Skepticism about the very possibility of truth in general is markedly different from a general skepticism held, as a kind of *a priori* policy, about the adequacy of this or that "truth." The first is paranoia, and the philosopher who holds to it is automatically a Cretan liar (in that he cannot claim that his claim is true). Skepticism of the second kind is often a good thing, and is the stuff of *scientia*. Of course, if Derrida is guilty of the first, radical nihilism, as his critics, and certain friends who disseminate Derrida's "nihilism," take him to be, we would have reason for alarm. For into the vacuum of unmeaning—which is to say, into the space left by the receding belief in the supportibility of "meaning" and "truth" and "presence" in principle—those who would instate, by naked power, a convenient kind of all three soon rush in. This history has shown many times; and the scandal that erupted in 1987 about Paul de Man's wartime activities, and his concomitant need to relativize language utterly, has not helped the Deconstructionist cause. I, however, do not find evidence of radical skepticism or nihilism in Jacques Derrida's writing; merely a caution about the dangers of logocentrism. That he has not shown us a way out himself, that he is as trapped by logocentrism as those he chides, should only make us seek elsewhere for adequate answers to questions of presence, meaning, and truth. And this with renewed urgency precisely because he has shown us the frailty of our language-bound tools.

13. In the library of built works since the 1500s, Robert Venturi finds no shortage of examples of the kinds of contradictions that Deconstruction also finds in texts. Venturi, after

all, was the author of the seminal *Complexity and Contradiction in Architecture* in 1966, and one could make the case that Deconstruction, as distinct from De- (read "neo-") constructivism, has its roots as a modern theory in architecture in Venturi's thought. This would make Venturi not only the "father" of postmodernism (in architecture) by virtue of his praise of irony, historicism, mannerism, and his devastating critique of the International Style, but also the father of Deconstructivism in his investigation of contradiction and conflict.

However, issues of self-consistency, self-reference, and the revelation of internal logical operations as such were not, and are not, part of Venturi's program. His "deconstructions" rested on the adoption of certain positive critical positions with respect to historical and contextual forces— issues, in a way, outside of the work and impinging upon it— as well as on the adoption of powerful normative notions about what good architecture *is* (which is to say, almost anything *but* "Orthodox Modern"). Venturi advocates ambiguity and pluralism on the grounds of the aesthetic *richness* and "levels of meaning" achievable, a pair of interests, of worthwhile ends, that Deconstruction ostensibly does not hold to.

Furthermore, convinced that architecture is a technologically simple art, Venturi sees no value in futurisms, and remains attached to mannerist, baroque, vernacular, and contextualist models of style. His praise of local inconsistency and perversity is thus largely seen at a compositional level— of facades, of plans—and is normalized by his equal praise of wholeness or resolution (his "difficult whole"), of conventions, and of the ultimate decidability/justification of meta-architectural issues. "Validity" is his oft-used word in this connection. Deconstruction, going deeper, leaves us without such resolution or the hope of it.

"In the end," Venturi writes in a retrospection of his seminal house for his mother, "I am speaking of a historicist symbolism that seeks the essence of style—or a place, of a tradition . . . for achieving essence is our ultimate aim in using symbolism in architecture . . ." (*A View from the Campidoglio* [New York: Harper, 1984] 118). Again, no Deconstructionist would admit to seeking essences.

It is also interesting to note Venturi's reliance on the New Critics of his day for his theoretical tools: T. S. Eliot, Cleanth Brooks, Stanley Edgar Hyman, William Empson, and Kenneth Burke. Contemporary Deconstructivists use Derrida,

Bloom, Foucault, Baudrillard, et al. in much the same way. One wonders if architectural theory will ever free itself from the linguistic analogy as an explanation of how architecture bears meaning. Nevertheless, a full study of Robert Venturi as a theorist and practitioner of Deconstruction deserves to be undertaken. It will surely involve a close reading of *Complexity and Contradiction* together with a new look at his architecture.

14. Cf. Bernard Tschumi, *Cinégramme Folie: Le Parc de la Villette*, (Princeton: Princeton Architectural P, 1988).

15. Jacques Derrida, *Writing and Difference*, trans. A. Bass (Chicago: Chicago UP, 1978) 259-260.
   Here is another passage, explicitly more architectural, from an essay by Derrida, "The Ends of Man" (a 1968 lecture printed in Baynes, Bohman, and McCarthy, eds., *After Philosophy* [Cambridge, MA: MIT P, 1987] 125-53). He is talking about alternative strategic options for humanist philosophy after Heidegger:

a. To attempt an exit and a deconstruction without changing terrain, by repeating what is implicit in the founding concepts and the original problematic, by using against the edifice the instruments or stones available in the house, that is, equally in language. Here one risks ceaselessly confirming, consolidating, relifting (relever), at an always more certain depth than which one allegedly deconstructs. The continuous process of making explicit, moving towards and opening, risks sinking into the autism of closure.

b. To decide to change terrain, in a discontinuous and irruptive fashion, by brutally placing oneself outside, and by affirming an absolute break and difference. Without mentioning all the other forms of trompe l'oeil *perspective in which such a displacement can be caught, thereby inhabiting more naively and more strictly than ever the inside one declares one has deserted, the simple practice of language ceaselessly reinstates the new terrain of the oldest ground. The effects of such a reinstatement or of such a blindness could be shown in numerous precise instances. (151)*

16. One hesitates to state the most obvious indication of some affinity between Derrida and architecture: his coining

of the word "deconstruction" in the first place. This word presents itself instantly as a provocative oxymoron about building and demolition, structure and failure—at least it does so to architects. I must assume that something similar went on in Derrida's mind, and that the provocation—the mixing of professions, so to speak—caught also the ears of philosophers. We hardly need to know—-indeed, it hurts to know—that "deconstruction" is an extension of the word *destruktion*, used by Heidegger to mean roughly the same thing.

17. The idea that text can be treated as an organism or building is central to the Judaic Kabbalistic tradition. The Torah, or Pentateuch, according to the Kabbalah, is not merely a fixed communication between God and man, but a living thing of infinite meaning, its letters "nothing less than configurations of the divine light." The Torah, says the Zohar (a part of the Kabbalah), "is like a building" or a human body, or the Tree of Life, with parts and aspects without end. The Torah is unfathomable divine speech itself, the meaning of which is "revealed differently at different levels and according to the capacity of its contemplator." Kabbalistic interpretations would often "deliberately choose to stress certain words or verses that seemed insignificant on the surface and attribute to them profound symbolic importance," a method, as we shall see, central to Deconstruction.

　　All quotatations in the above paragraph are from Gershom Sholem, *Kabbalah* (New York: Dorset, 1987) 168-174.

18. Derrida is not the first, or only, writer today to operate with a proto-architectural vocabulary of metaphors. For a study of this, see Susan Frank, *Literary Architecture* (Berkeley: California UP, 1979).

19. As this book went to press I received John M. Ellis's *Against Deconstruction* (Princeton: Princeton UP, 1989). It is the most eloquent, forceful, sustained, detailed, and damaging critique of Derrida's Deconstruction now available. (Previous ones have tended to be review articles by individuals such as Gerald Graff, Michael Fischer, Frederick Crews, and, of course, the late John Searle in the famous *Glyph* exchange with Derrida [1 & 2, 1977]). Readers of the present work will find many areas of agreement between myself and Ellis, his expressed as debunkings, and mine as reservations. Ellis does not deal with the architectural movement, how-

ever. Nor, in my view, does Ellis, in his determination to show that Deconstruction is neither new nor logically consistent, diagnose with sufficient appreciation what mystical—yet no less real—fire the smoke of Deconstruction issues from. This I have attempted to do.

20. My overall exposition of Derrida's ideas is guided by Jonathan Culler's account, in *On Deconstruction: Theory and Criticism after Structuralism* (New York: Cornell UP, 1982), on parts of Rodolphe Gasche's *The Tain of the Mirror* (Cambridge: Harvard UP, 1986), and on direct readings of certain of Derrida's essays in *Of Grammatology,* trans. G. C. Spivak (Baltimore: Johns Hopkins UP, 1974), *Margins of Philosophy,* trans. Alan Bass (Chicago: Chicago UP, 1982), *Positions,* trans. Alan Bass (Chicago: Chicago UP, 1981), and *Dissemination,* trans. Barbara Johnson (Chicago: Chicago UP, 1981). Other works by Derrida are cited as needed.

It should be noted that Culler is himself criticized by doctrinaire Deconstructionists (and anti-Deconstructionists!) for over-simplifying and normalizing Deconstruction. Making Deconstruction relatively clear and accessible tends to remove not only its sting and radicalism, but its involving, elite-producing difficulty. Nor am I alone in using Culler as a guide. A philosopher no less august than Jurgen Habermas does the same in his 1985 *The Philosophical Discourse of Modernity* that I will cite later.

21. Very few buildings and architects will in fact be used as demonstrations for the points to be made, and all are rather well known. For a plethora of candidates for illustrative use in discussing Deconstruction, the reader is directed to *Precedents in Architecture* by Roger Clark and Michael Pause (New York: Van Nostrand, 1985), where beginning analyses of hierarchical, geometrical, functional, and other patterns in "famous buildings" are made, and from which any number of deconstructive critical projects can be launched.

A note about usage in this essay. The term "Deconstruction" is capitalized when it refers to Derrida's body of thought, but when what is referred to is something you or I might do, perhaps having learned from Deconstruction, it is "deconstruction," with a small "d." The adjectival forms will be as follows: "Deconstructionist" for Derridean procedures, "Deconstructivist" for the purely architectural ones derived from the movement called Deconstructivism, while "deconstructive" remains ambiguous and depends on context for disambiguation. The verb "to deconstruct" and the rare adverbial form "deconstructively" likewise depend on context (otherwise we would end up with such ogres as "Deconstructivistically" and so on). There is no "Deconstructionism," just Deconstruction.

22. *Margins*, 7.

23. Eisenman, too, seems to see the parallel; see John Taylor, "Mr. In-Between." For a further explication of *ma,* see Gunther Nitschke, " 'Ma,' the Japanese Sense of Place," *Architectural Design* (March 1966): 116-56.

24. Derrida, it has often been observed, is carrying out a part of the Hegelian program. It was Hegel, with his dialectic method, his advocacy of skepticism, his emphasis on history and language, his acceptance of inherent contradictions in "higher forms" of logic, and his impact on Marx and all subsequent social theory in European thought, who set the context for Derrida.

However, the similarity is striking between Derrida's ("non-concept" denoted by the "non-word") *différance* and the doctrine of *zim-zum* of the Lurianic Kabbalah. *Zim-zum* is the primal "contraction" or "withdrawal" of God from identity with His creation, with Himself. With this contraction He leaves room for things, for life, for man, for phenomena. These all now inhabit a zone of traces, remnants, vessels, into which His substance only shines.

Of Kabbalistic influences on Hegel we know little; Hegel acknowledges the influence of Spinoza, and Spinoza was well acquainted with Kabbalistic doctrine of his day. (See Gershom Scholem, as well as Leo Schaya, *The Universal Meaning of the Kaballah*, trans. Nancy Pearson [New Jersey: University Books, 1971]).

One may also find remarks concordant with mine on the influence of Kabbalism on Derrida in Harold Bloom's *Kabbalah and Criticism* (New York: Seabury, 1975) 52, and in Imre Salusinzsky, *Criticism in Society* (New York: Methuen, 1987) 53, where Bloom, in an interview, cites himself (above) and remarks further. Also see Jurgen Habermas's essay "Beyond a Temporalized Philosophy of Origins: Jacques Derrida's Critique of Phonocentrism," in his *The Philosophical Discourse of Modernity* (Cambridge, MA: MITP, 1987)

161ff, and Susan Handelman "Jacques Derrida and the Heretic Hermeneutic," in M. Krupnic, ed., *Displacement, Derrida, and After* (Bloomington: Indiana UP, 1983) 98ff, which Habermas discusses in note 10 of his essay.

Finally, there are also distinct affinities between *différance* and certain Taoist and Mahayana Buddhist tenets— in particular, the doctrine of infinite negations. Discussion of the affinities of *différance* with either Western (Jewish) or Eastern (primarily Buddhist) mysticism, however, though eminently worthwhile, lie outside the scope of this essay, as would be yet one more affinity with the notion, from physics, of the *quantum field*—that invisible ground of active, energic nothingness from which everything real, splitting itself in two, particle and antiparticle, rhymelessly leaps and falls back in unimaginably complex ways—a connection, I believe, of which Derrida is fully, and cannily, aware.

For extended discussions, specifically of the concept of *différance*, see David Wood and Robert Bernasconi, eds., *Derrida and Différance* (Evanston, IL: Northwestern UP, 1988).

25. In the *Tao Te Ching* (chapter 2) we read:

When the people of the world all know beauty as beauty,
There arises the recognition of ugliness.
When they all know the good as good,
There arises the recognition of evil.
Therefore:
Being and non-being produce each other;
Difficult and easy complete each other;
Long and short contrast each other;
High and low distinguish each other;
Sound and voice harmonize each other;
Front and behind accompany each other.

(Trans. Wing-Tsit Chan, New York: Macmillan, 1985)

Things get more difficult, however, when the "oppositions" one is considering are of a different sort from left/right, or cause/effect—for example, nature/culture, or speaking/writing. Derrida's arguments are full of such groupings of oppositions, all of which, by listing them together as further examples and ending in "etc.," he treats as having the same logical status as that of black/white, and the rest. We find ourselves contemplating whether, for example, we can have *nature* without *culture,* or *speaking* without *writing.*

That the answer to these may be "no" is startling, to say the least. It is just this kind of reversal that Derrida asks us to execute. And indeed, it can be argued that without culture—that is, without a "you" and an "I" thinking and communicating in a language and for a reason—nature would not need to be pointed out as "nature." When *everything* is nature, there is no "nature." Thus the existence of "nature" as a category of thought, and therefore as a set of phenomena of a certain sort, is predicated on the existence of culture. Similarly with cause and effect. One experiences the effect and then looks for a cause, does one not? The naming/experiencing proceeds in reverse order to the logical presentation. And writing, if one allows pre-phonetic and pre-ideographic inscription and gesture to be "writing," may indeed be logically parallel to, if not prior to, speech utterances. And so on.

This style of arguing, however, can be very philological rather than logical, and merely logical rather than scientific in the best, inquiring sense of the word. It is essentially a dialectical procedure (I say "essentially" because Derrida, unlike Hegel, never poses a transcendental solution, the "higher, third term" that would dissolve the tension). If the dialectic of "undecidables" (Derrida's word) is an *un*acceptable general procedure, then one has a legitimate gripe with the whole of Deconstruction, built as it is upon such arguments. Derrida, in his own logocentric way, is not very careful to distinguish between different types of "opposition": logical inverses, formal converses, ends of continua, single dimensional, multi-dimensional, whole or partial, and so on. The ways of "reversing" terms, ideas, and shapes are many in number. Without going into the nature of "opposition" deeply, therefore, the best strategy is to become that much more cautious, granting Derrida his reversals and inversions only one at a time, according to what the components are logically, empirically, and historically, and how they might be understood, as far as possible, aside from the nature of language.

26. And what of our own, individual *presence*? Is the sense of it not enhanced, indeed constituted, by the ongoing possibility of our absence, our death? One need not be a scholar of Heidegger, Camus, or Sartre to appreciate this ancient truth.

For remarks by Derrida on the profound influence of

Sartre upon his education see Wood and Bernasconi, *Derrida and Différance,* 75.

27. Derrida, quoted in Culler, *On Deconstruction,* 85, 86.

28. This is another whole essay. Wright's use of glass is instructive: the more he made it go away—eliminating the frame, cutting it directly into stone and brick as at Fallingwater—the more keenly, of course, it stayed.

29. For a short discussion of this kind of "erasure" by Heidegger and Derrida, see G. C. Spivak's Preface to *Of Grammatology,* xv-xviii.

Notice that we are *not* here retelling Laotse's famous lines from the *Tao Te Ching,* 119:

Thirty spokes are united around the hub to make a wheel,
But it is on their non-being that the utility of the
carriage depends.
Clay is molded to form a utensil,
But it is on its non-being that the utility of the
utensil depends.
Doors and windows are cut out to make a room,
But it is on its non-being that the utility of the
room depends.
Therefore turn being into advantage, and non-being
into utility.

which, true and beautiful as they are, are more about the synergy of parts, about elements which, in their being-together, create further "beings" we may well find useful and quite real, but which, like one's "lap" or one's "fist," would evaporate if the constituent elements were reconfigured, unfolded or disintegrated. Nor are we talking about the powerful presence of simple openings in, say, huge monolithic walls, or of cavities in general. Rather, we are talking about the absence that co-exists with, and suffuses, the present object; a sort of condition that arises from either, or both, our questioning *and* the object's self-questioning. Jean Paul Sartre's discussion in the early chapter on "negation" in *Being and Nothingness* is without parallel in exploring the issue.

30. Ludwig Mies van der Rohe, cited in Wolf Tegethoff, *Mies van der Rohe: The Villas and Country Houses* (New York:

MoMA, 1985) 67, and in Philip Johnson, *Mies van der Rohe* (New York: MoMA, 1947) 182. I am grateful for both quotations and a number of other insights about Mies for this paper to Caroline Constant and her paper "The Barcelona Pavilion as Landscape Garden: Modernity and the Picturesque" (manuscript, 1989).

31. *Positions*: 41ff.

32. For a full discussion of such "levels of description" and the notion of "depth" in architectural meaning-systems, I can only commend to the reader chapter 4 of my book *The Dimension of Depth: An Inquiry through Architecture* (forthcoming).

33. One might here use a term in English that offers opportunities for punning similar to those offered to Derrida by "*difference*," and that is the term "*distinction.*" Distinction can mean quite simply "difference," as when one object or idea is distinct from another. *Distinction* also implies honor, special presence, valorization, however, as when we speak of someone being distinguished, or of distinctive suite, and so on.

34. I suppose one is led to wonder whether Bohr's statement is profoundly or trivially true. Anecdote cited by Benno Schmidt in "The Freshman Address," *The Yale Alumni Magazine* (October 1988): 56.

35. Culler, *On Deconstruction*, 248.

36. Walter Michaels, cited in Culler, *On Deconstruction*, 232.

37. Ibid.

38. Derrida's recently translated and perhaps most accessible work, *Of Spirit*, discusses the suppression and re-expression of the notion of spirit in Heidegger, and provides another apt example.

Much simplified: Here Derrida shows how the rather conventional, mystic idea of "spirit" *(Geist)*, which in *Sein und Zeit* Heidegger had warned his readers at length against employing in establishing the unique character of his *Dasein* and which he proceeded assiduously to avoid using without quotation marks until 1933 and his influential *Rectorship*

Address, in fact is a suppressed presence throughout Heidegger's writing, a hidden factor. After 1933, the quotation marks are removed, and Heidegger came to be "read," indeed began to read himself, politically, as endorsing the spirit of the people—*der Volk*—in terms of Will and Destiny toward unification with Being. Hegelian "folk spirit" and crypto-Christian "spirituality," once suppressed, now emerge redoubled in strength, it seems, and well suited to the National Socialist agenda.

See Jacques Derrida, *Of Spirit: Heidegger and the Question*, trans. Geoffrey Bennington and Rachel Bowlby (Chicago: Chicago UP, 1989).

39. To my mind, the matter of *espacement*, or "spacing," treated this abstractly and generically, however, precludes it from doing anything truly interesting. With all this, Eisenman ends by *illustrating* Deconstruction, as though giving us a lesson, a diagram, without actually deconstructing anything. This contentlessness is not something Eisenman is ashamed of. He does not concede "meaning" to architecture in the first place, other than or outside of its moves in self-reference. See Peter Eisenman, "The Futility of Objects: Decomposition and the Processes of Difference," *Harvard Architecture Review* 3 (1984): 65-81.

40. See John Whiteman, "Site Unscene—Notes on Architecture and the Concept of Fiction," *AA Files* 12, 76-84; Peter Eisenman, "The Authenticity of Difference: Architecture and the Crisis of Reality," *Center: A Journal for American Architecture* 4 (1988): 50-57, and Robert Mugerauer, "Derrida and Beyond," in the same issue, 66-75.

41. Venturi, in *Complexity and Contradiction:*

Louis Kahn has referred to "what a thing wants to be," but implicit in this statement is its opposite: what the architect wants the thing to be. In the tension and balance between these two lie many of the architect's decisions. (13)

In this proto-Deconstructionist passage we have three metaphorizations of opposition: tension, balance, and implicitness (etymologically: "folded-in"-ness). The last is especially Deconstructionist. The *opposite* is imagined lodged silently inside, parasitically, perhaps generatively, or swirled inextricably into its body, at any rate, a difference achieved by a contest of containment. We find visual analogs—picturings—of all three in Venturi's built work, as one might expect.

42. See George Lakoff and Mark Johnson, *Metaphors We Live By* (Chicago: Chicago UP, 1980) for an excellent review of this.

43. Daniel Libeskind, in Wigley and Johnson, 34.

44. It is interesting to compare Libeskind's words here with those of Carlo Carra on Futurism:

We reject the right angle, which we call passionless, cube and pyramid, all static forms . . . We want the shock of all acute angles, we want the dynamic arabesque, the slanted lines which attack the senses of the spectator like arrows falling from the sky; the whirling circle, the ellipse, the spiral, the upside down cone—the shape of explosion; we want the polyphonic and polyrythmic shapes which correspond to an need for inner disharmony." ("La Pittura dei Suoni," Archivi del Futurismo, Rome: 1958) vol 1, 74; cited in Alfred Neumeyer, *The Search for Meaning in Modern Art*, trans. R. Angress (Englewood Cliffs: Prentice, 1964) 84.

One would hope that the study of Deconstruction would inject a maximum of subtlety and precision into the revival of the formal gestures of Constructivism, Futurism, and Suprematism in the 1980s and 90s.

45. As for the imagery he uses to describe what he is doing—now mechanical, now biological, now playful, now deadly—this is par for the Deconstructionist rhetorical course. But tracking/attacking what? Should one deconstruct this text rather than his project?

46. This taxonomy is of my own formulation but is implicit in the work of Louis Kahn. An expansion of this taxonomy, and the reasoning behind it, is found in my *The Dimension of Depth*. Abbreviated use of it is made later in this essay.

47. Inside/outside has received no better examination that I

know of than in Venturi's *Complexity and Contradiction*.

48. See Steven Peterson, "Space and Anti-Space," *Harvard Architecture Review* 1 (Spring 1980): 89-113.

49. At other times, Le Corbusier gives equal and oppositely extreme emphasis to the roof as *roof*, something in its own right, at the Heidi Weber Pavilion, and at Ronchamps. At Ronchamps, the opposition of flotation/flying and weight/solidity is fully deployed, while at the Pavilion the means of support is almost fully dissimulated.

50. It may be argued that the column began as a rare and sacred object with the Sumerians, and then the Minoans; that the Greeks, in fact, by appropriating and repeating it, thus "quoting" it, devalued its sacrality. The "classical" column becomes meaningful now through its very stability, iterability, and iteration, as Derrida would want to say, but meaningful in a different way, that is, referentially. The Romans were thus twice removed from original meaning, and we moderns four or five times removed. Derrida would explain that there was no original meaning, that the process of "quotation" by replication and re-use in new contexts goes back indefinitely far in time, past culture, past nature, past physics, to *différance,* the same *différance* that still energizes its presence relative to the not-column.

51. Derrida would say that such repressions are *logically* necessary, as a manifestation of *différance*.

Most level-headed and good-hearted architects would reject this notion, however. They imagine the possibility of "having it all," in what Venturi called a "difficult whole" at least, if not in some grand unity. What is at stake here is enormous: namely, architects' pride in the all-conquering, all-resolving effectiveness of pure creativity in arriving at a design "solution." Failure to pay democratic attention to all components of the taxonomy is just that, failure: failure to be sufficiently creative, failure to be patient, failure to have studied the problem in sufficient detail.

Of course, there are realists. Realists understand the constraints of talent and time that confront the architect, and they know that perfection is not practically possible. But even they, I think, would be unwilling to exclude the very *possibility* of evenhandedness, in principle. They are apt to imagine that great buildings are examples of complete expression of all taxonomic elements. They would be wrong, of course. Architects, all architects, *must* choose this over that for the gift of presence.

If Derrida, on the one hand (and as his critics claim) seeks to de-legitimize through his Deconstruction any valorization or choice, while, on the other hand, evolution and design depend on "collapsing the wave function," that is, on the "tragic yet beautiful sacrifice of the plenum of indeterminacy for identity" (Alex Argyros, personal communication), then we must depart from Derrida. But Derrida, in my view, is not saying this at all. He is saying only that choice leaves its marks.

Thus, in a paradoxical turn, the architect in search of ever greater completeness of concern and choicelessness of expression indeed finds both: inevitably, repressed material finds its way to the surface somehow, and does its work in rising up. This is as true of every interesting building as it is of every interesting text.

52. I hate to do this, but Venturi is as guilty as anyone of hit-and-run appreciation/criticism. *Complexity and Contradiction* contains over 300 illustrations of almost as many buildings, perhaps no more than ten of which receive more than a sentence of commentary.

For a critique complementary to mine in these last paragraphs, see also James Marston Fitch, "Experiential Context of Aesthetic Process," *Journal of Architectural Education* 41: 2 (Winter 1988): 4-9.

53. It fits well with the whole post-structuralist/Marxist thrust, especially via Foucault.

54. Central hearths in the Nordic tradition, and as adopted by Wright, are an example. Hurricane, tornado, and bombing-raid protection consists in finding the heart of the house, that place both farthest from the outside and most contained by structure, or the basement, that *deepest* part in the sense of downwardness and embeddedness.

55. For a fuller discussion of this phenomenon, see my *The Dimension of Depth: An Inquiry through Architecture*.

56. Wall surface treatments such as fresco, or wallpaper, or

intense materiality and color, are an exception to the rule of marginality; unless one considers the wall in its section, in which case the whole wall surface is marginal with respect to what penetrates the wall, and room, interiors.

57. See Jacques Derrida, *The Truth in Painting*, trans. G. Bennington and I. McLeod (Chicago: Chicago UP, 1987).

There is also a relationship to be explored between Derrida's *parergon* and the notion of *keys* and *keying* in Irving Goffman's excellent *Frame Analysis* (Cambridge: Harvard UP, 1974). Keying is the information we receive that announces how the social situation we are about to partake in is to be understood. Keys "tune us in" to what's "going on." Keys mark, frame, announce and introduce us. Much of the comedy of errors, as well as many tragedies, depend upon mischief and mis-takes with keys: and both will continue to be viable dramatic forms as long as visible sets of behaviors and statements make "perfect sense" under a number of construals of the nature of the situation, which is to say, indefinitely.

58. . . . such as this one, dear good reader, Reader of Footnotes. You enter the text below the text, the alter-text. Perhaps you have by now decided which is more important: that one which others race along and upon above, promising themselves to return but who likely never will, having consigned these words to the shadows; or this ongoing conversation, here, linked up under the streets of assertion.

59. A fact curiously unremarked upon by the editors of *Reconstruction/Deconstruction*.

60. In this hermeticism it shares something with New Criticism and opposes the Frye-an Romantic modes.

61. See Culler, *On Deconstruction,* 123 for more on "context."

62. In analogous fashion, physicists may place their particle accelerators anywhere, and (in principle) use any matter as a supply of protons and neutrons to "smash."

63. Again we find Derrida deploying Kabbalistic doctrine. Augustine held that the world was God's Book. To understand

nature and the order of creation was to read and interpret the largest Scripture of all. Kabbalism turns the equivalence around: instead of the world being God's Book, the Book is God's World, that is, *the* world. This sets the stage for looking within texts, or, rather, within "textuality" itself, for truth and revelation. (Some mention of this theme was made in note 12 above with regard to the status of the Torah in Kabbalist Judaism. Cf. also Derrida's essay on Edmond Jabés in *Writing and Difference*, especially p. 76, where he writes: "One emerges from the book only within the book, because, for Jabés, the book is not in the world, the world is in the book.") Implied is the forsaking of action, of empirical observation, and of the natural sciences that depend on it.

And indeed it seems often to turn out this way today. Poststructuralists in general seem more than happy to portray the "hard sciences" if not as fictions, then as dependent on textuality for their very continuance. (See Richard Rorty, *Consequences of Pragmatism* [Chicago: Chicago UP, 1982] 90-109 and 139-59.) *Logos,* meaning reason, is subsumed by *logos,* meaning word. The possibility of non-verbal logic and of non-verbal meaning is wished away, obliterated, by the presumed hegemony of language in thought.

Derrida struggles in the infinite web of logocentrism, knowing it is a web, telling us it is a web, but will not leap from it, though he has leapt from it with every metaphor whose meaning can no longer be carried in words, which is to say, almost every metaphor he uses.

64. A difficult word to translate: perhaps "cozy conviviality," "comfortableness," "ease." Herr Baumann, the commercial artist client for Coop Himmelblau's Atelier Baumann in Vienna, speaks of his environment as a "bomb" set in the heart of pompous and self-satisfied Viennese architecture (personal communication, 1987).

65. This is the best way to understand Robert Venturi's National Gallery, as well as a number of his other works that are both contextual and critical.

For a rendition of the idea of critical realism, see Kenneth Frampton, "Ten Points on an Architecture of Regionalism: A Provisional Polemic," *Center: A Journal for Architecture in America* 3 (1987): 20-27.

66. "I like repetition: it is as if the future trusted in us, as if

it waited for us, encoded in an ancient word—which hasn't yet been given voice." Jacques Derrida, in Wood and Bernasconi, *Derrida and Différance*, 81.

67. The reader should be aware that the argument that follows is to a large extent my own and not Derrida's, or anyone else's, although it comes close to certain theories of the origins of language centered on mimicry. Cf. Roger Wescott, ed., *Language Origins* (Maryland: Linstock, 1974), especially 207-12, a commentary by John L. Fischer. Cf. also R. W. Mitchell, N. S. Thompson, eds., *Deception: Perspectives on Human and Nonhuman Deceit* (Albany: State U of New York P, 1986), especially 221ff.

68. Derrida's notion of *s'entendre parler*, or "hearing/understanding oneself speak" picks up only after language is established. "At the moment of one's own speech," as Culler, elucidating *s'entendre parler,* phrases it, ". . .signified and signifier seem simultaneously given, . . . inside and outside, material and spiritual seem fused, (and this moment) serves as a point of reference in relation to which all these essential distinctions can be posited" [*On Deconstruction,* 107]. Speech seems both originary and transparent to meanings, a model of presence, Derrida notes, while in truth it is neither. Camille would not argue. (If she could "argue" at all, that is. On second thought, if she could argue, she might well.) Her realizations of the efficacy of speech or, for that matter, the efficacy of any displaceable and iterable gesture, must begin in problematicity and experiment, the gap between signifier and signified wide and uncertain.

69. Umberto Eco, *A Theory of Semiotics* (Bloomington: Indiana UP, 1976) 7; cited in Culler, *On Deconstruction,* 114.
    Derrida, as one might expect, goes further, positing a deep and ineradicable relationship between *duplication* and *duplicity.* See Gasche, 225ff.

70. *Dissemination*, 168.

71. I said "perhaps" at the beginning of the paragraph because it is difficult, objectively, to confirm our intuition of intentionality in this case. For an account of the sad history of theories of language origins, see James H. Stam, *Inquiries into the Origins of Language* (New York: Harper, 1976).

72. I do not have the room here to argue the point thoroughly. The linguistic/semiotic account of architectural meaning is deeply entrenched in the current architectural *episteme*. The work required to reveal its shortcomings and undo its damage is only beginning. See my *The Dimension of Depth*.

73. One must also temporarily exclude the kind of iterations that have to do with the extreme and blind repetitions of mass-production, the repetitions that so exercised Walter Benjamin. To call instances of this repetition meaningful on account of their membership in the class of repeatables seems to go beyond the point of usefulness here.

Intuitively, we believe that proliferation demeans, that the spirit of the original is diluted, if not stolen, with each copy. All of Jean Baudrillard's lamentations for our age seem to derive from this ancient and superstitious feeling. In Derrida too we can detect a slightly withering regard for "simulacra" (a word which seems to have "mere" contained right in it), and when *we* read, dismayed, of dissemination as the truth of things, it is the same emotion that rises up. As though *one* of anything could make sense! At a certain level, without simulacra, without dissemination, without massive iterations, there could *be* nothing, certainly nothing physical. Uniqueness is a function of complexity and context, not of aloneness or singularity of essence. And it is in complexity and context that, in modern life and letters, we should look for our "units of meaning."

74. The parallel process in human behavior is often amusing, the stuff of many a comedy routine. It ties in well with Koestler's notion of humor as the playing off of mechanical and uncontrollable behaviors against the intentional, controlled behaviors that support man's claim to dignity.

75. Yet another direction for the argument lies in explicating, in part, the art of Marcel Duchamp, Man Ray, and other Dadaists and Surrealists, depending as they did on the dislocation and re-contextualization of everyday objects to achieve their odd claim on our attention. By appropriating them into the world of Art, the structure, shape, and very existence of the Artworld was revealed no less surely than the nature of the objects themselves. With this radical invention, Art—specifically modern art—was established to be a game of intentions

and the readings thereof. And this it has been ever since.

76. From Latin, *re* = again, *parire* = to bring forth.

77. Although one may sense the iterability of the pattern in general.

78. For where this kind of postmodernism has led of late, cf. Patricia Leigh Brown, "Disney Deco" and Paul Goldberger "And Now, an Architectural Kingdom," both in *The New York Times Magazine* (April 8, 1990): 18-24, where Goldberger concludes:

It is in Disney that the worlds of architecture and entertainment, which have been moving closer to each other for years, have achieved their most powerful intersection yet—becoming so intimately intertwined that it is sometimes impossible to tell which is which. It is a convergence that already means a lot for Disney, and it may turn out in the end to mean even more for architecture.

79. The failure of books that purport to explain architectural meaning is legendary. Almost all discourses about architectural meaning evaporate the moment one asks *what* is meant. Instead, more or less lyrical, more or less technical, descriptions of the building are put forward, describing every move and effect, and, at the moment we are ready to read what it all *means:* "The next morning . . ."

80. Peter Dews, from his review of *Dissemination* in the *New Statesman*, which reappears on the back cover "blurb" of the 1981 Chicago UP softcover edition.

81. *Dissemination*, 357.

82. Ibid. 241.

83. Cf. George Lakoff and Mark Johnson, *Metaphors We Live By,* for an extended discussion of the "grounding" and structure of metaphor.

84. *Writing and Difference*, trans. Alan Bass (Chicago: Chicago UP, 1978) 17. See also Derrida's essay "White Mythology: Metaphor in the Text of Philosophy" in *Margins of Philoso-*

phy, trans. Alan Bass (Chicago: U of Chicago P, 1982) 207-72. Here Derrida is concerned with showing the inextricability of metaphor from philosophy, while showing also that no critique or theory of this fact can use other than metaphorical means. Thus, "logical priority" is given to none—and all—and again we are left with movement and play only. As a "foundationalist" of sorts, of course, I argue that not all metaphors are equally deep, and that there is structure and priority to them, to their referential content and their own structuring, all the way "down" to the mathematical metaphors Derrida claims, for reasons I cannot find him stating, are not truly metaphors. (The last steps of hermeneutics are always to be taken outside of language and writing and speech, and with non-verbal thought strategies. Derrida stops at the gate. This is why he denies metaphoricity to the purely mathematical.)

It is often observed that metaphors divide into two classes: "active" and "inactive," that is, ones that are shaped and posed more or less freshly by the author in order to delight and/or facilitate comprehension, and ones that are so old, so idiomatic, so worn into practical language's figures of speech and even words, that they pass unnoticed as metaphors. Needless to say, Derrida reverses the active/ inactive hierarchy. So do George Lakoff and Mark Johnson *(Metaphors We Live By)*, but with no word toward Deconstruction (in fact, in a decidedly structuralist work). For both systems, however, "inactive," all but invisible, metaphors are precisely the ones through which the bulk of language's meanings pass.

85. When Louis Kahn says "what has been will always be," he does not mean that what will be is *only* that which always has been. He precludes erasure of the traces of the past, but not new growth, evolution, or elaboration upon them.

86. This date refers to the establishment of Jericho as the first true town.

87. The artist, said Plato, "besides producing any kind of artificial thing . . . can create all plants and animals, himself included, and earth and sky and gods and the heavenly bodies and all things under the earth and Hades." *Republic*, B. Jowett, ed., (New York: Oxford UP, 1945) 325.

This particular citation of Plato appears in a recent paper

that just came to my attention and which accords well with what I am driving at here: Robert Emmett Mueller, "Mnemesthetics: Art as the Revivification of Significant Consciousness Events," *Leonardo* 21: 2 (1988): 191-94.

88. See *Of Grammatology*, 9: "And thus we say 'writing' for all that gives rise to an inscription in general, whether it is literal or not, and even if what it distributes in space is alien to the order of the voice. . . ." This crucial passage is too long to reproduce here.

89. Stanley Tigerman's *The Architecture of Exile* (New York: Rizzoli, 1988) constitutes an exploration of the idea of Western architecture as arising from displacement: from Eden; from the place of the Hebrew covenant with Jahweh described in the last chapters of the book of Exodus; and from the site of Solomon's temple described in Kings I.

A much broader, and more anthropological, analysis on the theme of architecture not just as accommodation in the conventional sense but as the incomplete *accommodation to* foreignness—climatic and/or cultural—has yet to be accomplished.

90. "For buried in such conventional symbolism lies a natural symbolism, which speaks to those willing to listen" (40). Karsten Harries, in his article "The Voices of Space," *Center* 4 (1988): 49, argues along lines similar to those presented here, asking for an excavation of architecture's *arche-symbols.*

91. "Heidegger redux," one might comment here with some rue; especially since, as Derrida was a former student of Heidegger, his whole program might be interpreted as the Bloomian undoing/redoing of the master, *On Spirit* being but the latest example, and one with an uncharacteristically political dimension. For Martin Heidegger was a philosopher of "pure presence" par excellence, *the* seeker—next to Husserl—of absolute *essences* and *origins,* of the ineffable, ground-zero, unity of Being, and *the* advocate of authenticity, "peoplehood," at-homeness, spirituality, and earthiness, presented in a Promethean amalgam of difficult ideas and figures of speech. All these Derrida mercilessly sabotages throughout his writing (in language, unfortunately, no less idiosyncratic, obtuse, meditative, and self-reflexive), as

though to scatter and confuse the advance of any such meta-physics so totalizing, so self-certain, and at the same time so amoral and ungraspable as that of Heidegger's.

But of course, these last few pages have not been repre-sentations of Derrida's thought but of mine. They amount to the proposition that in the idea of "levels of meaning," prop-erly understood, there can be found a reconciliation of what is of value to architects in both the Heideggerian and Der-ridean perspectives. Later in this essay, for example, I shall speak of the necessary "abrasion" of levels and the canny ac-ceptance/avoidance of naturalism found in Louis Kahn, how at the Kimbell one finds everywhere *both* the "rhetoric" of authenticity and the undermining—the deconstruction—of that rhetoric. This is as it should be with architecture.

(Heidegger, we should note, has had, and continues to have, a strong influence on architectural thought, principal-ly through the writings of Christian Norberg-Shulz and Robert Mugerauer and chiefly in response to his essay "Building, Dwelling, Thinking" in *Poetry, Language, Thought*. I must also include my own *For an Architecture of Reality* as among works influenced by Heidegger. If nothing else, Derrida provides the salutary antidote.)

92. For a guide to the building, see Louis Kahn, *Light Is the Theme: Louis I. Kahn and the Kimbell Art Museum, Com-ments on Architecture by Louis Kahn,* compiled by Nell E. Johnson (Forth Worth: Kimbell Art Foundation, 1975); *In Pursuit of Quality: The Kimbell Art Museum* (Fort Worth: Kimbell Art Museum, 1987), and Patricia Loud, *The Art Mu-seums of Louis I. Kahn* (Durham: Duke UP, 1989). Brief doc-umentations of and references to the Kimbell abound in his-tories of modern architecture. The original construction drawings, upon which some of the observations in this essay are based, are held at the Drawings Collection of the Battle Hall Library at the University of Texas at Austin.

For critical/interpretive readings of the Kimbell that com-plement and often enlarge upon the critical reading pre-sented here, I recommend the essays by Doug Suisman, Dana Cuff, Peter McCleary, and Patricia Loud in *Design Book Review* 11 (Winter 1987): 35-55. The reader will also find ref-erences to further sources of historiographical interest.

93. "Crucial refinements": in everyday architectural practice, with the skepticism of everyday clients, crucial refinement is

all too often perceived as oxymoronic. The Derridean perspective on marginality and centrality makes us all the more sensitive.

94. For a fairly extended account of the commissioning, designing, and making of the Kimbell, see Patricia Loud, *The Art Museums of Louis I. Kahn*.

95. Of course, the open-ended and infinite nature of space was a Modernist invocation, as was the later idea of dotting such space with random-seeming "incidents."

96. Marshall Meyers, in an interview printed in *Louis Kahn,* a special issue of *A+U Architecture and Urbanism* 11 (1983): 225.

97. Of course, there are precedents for the repeated vault configuration within the canon of architecture, not only in any number of Roman baths and basilicas, but from Boulée's drawing of an extension to the Bibliothèque Nationale (1780), where the apex is opened up for light, to specific works by Le Corbusier: the Vaucresson weekend villa, his sketches for the Monol house, and for a house near Cherchell in North Africa. For a thorough discussion of all this, see Patricia Loud, "A History of the Kimbell Art Museum," *In Pursuit of Quality: The Kimbell Art Museum* and *The Art Museums of Louis I. Kahn*. Loud's extensive contribution to these beautifully produced volumes spells out much of the historical and technical material only suggested in this essay. Also see Lawrence Speck, "Evaluation: The Kimbell Art Museum," *AIA Journal* 71 (August 1982): 36-43.

98. Neither museum director Edmund Pillsbury nor architect Romaldo Giurgola, a former colleague of Kahn's at Pennsylvania, could have foreseen the strength of the opposition to the addition (essentially merely adding two more rows of perfectly matching vaults, north and south, to the existing building) from the architectural and art community. Pillsbury decided not to go ahead with the plan. The two considerations that seemed to have prevailed were, firstly, that the Kimbell had manifestly become an art object no less great than the art objects it contained, no *parergon* but an *"ergon,"* and, secondly, the simple fact that angering the high-culture community per se was not a good idea for a mu-

seum, whatever the merits of the case.

Most of the other arguments revolved around whether Giurgola's iterative and imitative scheme was respectful or "a vulgar mimicry that would blur the distinction between Kahn's masterwork and the later additions." (Paul Goldberger, "Kimbell Says Its Home Is a Treasure to Cherish," *The New York Times* [February 28, 1990]: B4). Pillsbury had argued strongly that the Kimbell's mission was to *serve* the needs of its growing collection and larger community. The building had to expand simply in order accommodate demand. He had pointed to any number of famous additions to famous museums. Why not his?

Of course, in the current cultural climate it is difficult to challenge the value of *service to the community* (service to a collection is a more abstruse notion). The fact is that more people at an expanded Kimbell would in and of itself, by the sheer number of bodies—voices, faces, feet, and T-shirts—by the wear and tear, by the greater traffic of the stairs, porches, bookshop, and bathrooms, have undone the character of the building-in-use as it now stands, that is to say, the building's dignity, peace, and relative emptiness.

Whether Giurgola's solution, doubling the gallery area, was stylistically correct (or even technically possible) or not, is ultimately beside the point. Yes, Kahn's Kimbell was a design that spoke of repetition and non-finiteness, of self-quotation and practicality, yes, earlier schemes for the Kimbell had a larger number of vaults (interestingly always three rows, never five, as Giurgola proposed) but, as any engineer will tell you, adding more of any function to a machine—more horsepower, more weight, more parts, more space—stresses the entire machine. If the machine is not designed in advance to be augmented, breakdown—partial or total—is likely.

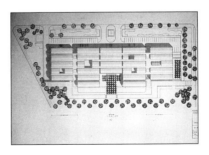

Romaldo Giurgola, proposed additions to the Kimbell, site plan.

The duplication and dissemination of ideas, of words and texts and images, of pure information, may proceed without cost to the original (should there meaningfully *be* an original, *pace* Derrida and Baudrillard), and it may even increase the original's value (*pace* Walter Benjamin). Architecture, it would seem, is a "horse of a different feather" (*pace* Walt Kelly); firstly, one where the extension of an original by duplication is typically seen as a failure of design ingenuity, but, secondly, one where if the functionality of the extended building is to remain integral, new physical and energic stresses are put into play throughout. The growth dynamics of texts and image systems, weightless, intrinsically proliferative, are quite different.

See also Paul Goldberger, "Sincerest Flattery or the Subtlest Form of Dishonor," *The New York Times* (September 24, 1989): H33; Mimi Swartz, "Kimbell Conundrum," *Texas Monthly* (March 1990); "Kimbell Art Museum Master Plan: Preserving the Past by Looking Ahead," including Architect's Statement, Design Approach and Program, (mimeo, Kimbell Art Museum, 1990).

99. Under Paul Cret at the University of Pennsylvania in the 1930s. Cret also influenced George Howe, who was trained at the Ecole des Beaux-Arts in Paris. Kahn and Howe were partners in the 1940s and again in the 50s.

100. Of course, as one might expect, Kahn's love of Roman architecture was not confined, or even concentrated, on its temples and civic structures, but rather embraced its engineering works: roads and aqueducts, ports, baths, and quotidian housing. For some remarkable formal similarities to the Kimbell see Geoffrey Rickman, *Roman Granaries and Store Buildings* (New York: Cambridge UP, 1971), especially the *horrea* at Patara and Myra (138, 139). The narrow, barrel-vaulted room, arranged in rows, was typical of Roman storehouse design, and certainly would have become evident to Kahn on his trips to Ostia.

101. The full plan of the Trenton Bath Houses also shows this form, much earlier.

102. Preceding the Kimbell, at the Salk Institute at La Jolla, I believe we see Kahn beginning the process of "de-hierarchization," decentralization, of repetition begun and ended

without announcement, as though for practical reasons. There is a powerful central axis through the Salk Institute, to be sure, but note how it is empty—a thin watercourse through a desolate plaza. Note also that its ends are unresolved classically (with a statue or special view, say) but rather are swept away, leaving us hanging in space, in desire, in wondering what is being pointed to. With his last building, the British Art Center in New Haven, another museum, we see Kahn again investigating the antihierarchical schema further. We witness the absence of center or culmination, and the cellular field of repetition is simply curtailed at street's edge.

A further note with regard to the collaborativeness and pragmatism described earlier is appropriate here. Kahn's "genius" as such is not reasonably at question in the making of the Kimbell or any of his buildings. We only confront again one of the central mysteries of the discipline: how any architect, through a tumble of practicums and accidents, through opportunism and not-always-amicable collaboration, both invokes and transcends necessity.

103. See Sarah Rossbach, *Feng Shui: The Chinese Art of Placement* (New York: Dutton, 1983), for a general review; also R. G. H. Siu, *Ch'i* (Cambridge, MA: MIT P, 1974).

104. These are internal dimensions.

105. Asking brick "what it wants to be"—perhaps Kahn's most quotable quote—entails not *letting* brick be what it wants to be, which is a pile, but challenging it to be as *much* as it can be, within in its nature, as one might challenge a child.

106. One is led to this reflection:

The terms "structure" and "theory of structures" in common architectural parlance refer not to anything abstract but to that set of elements of a building that give it its stiffness and strength against the forces of gravity, wind, and so on. As old as architecture itself and only recently shared (some would say co-opted) by the discipline of engineering, the discourse that contains our expertise on these matters analyzes a building according to a finite scheme of structural *types*—a vocabulary, if you will—of rigid configurations, elements, that may be arranged in ways constrained by, and ultimately validated by, not any resultant *sense,* or meaningfulness, but the actual, observable strength and stiffness of buildings. Open any book on structures and you will find them: the Beam, the Arch, the Truss, the Vault, the Buttress, the Retaining Wall, the Slab (One Way and Two Way), and so on.

Of course, the building itself knows no such categories. Nor does it stand up on account of their existence thus circumscribed. This is patently clear when we watch a building being demolished. It does not come apart in textbook pieces; rather, it hangs on to itself in all kinds of unlikely shapes, expressing all kinds of unlikely alliances between parts and regions of its material fabric. The same is clear when a building is under construction, when its physical parts—propped, stressed, and pinned this way and that— are called upon to cooperate in ways that are instantly compromising of their correct usage, indeed of their *raison d'être* as themselves.

Construction and demolition are temporary states; they are not the normal case, one might say, and one should not "build a case" upon them. But in fact, a real building—in place, built, connected, functioning—also distributes its forces in patterns that only approximate, if not defy, the purity of the textbook "elements of structure." For all but the most minimal of structures, or a structure deliberately shaped and isolated *as* a canonical element, there exists a considerable complexity and an ineradicable indeterminacy about how it is actually behaving, about where the forces and energies are actually going. Alternative structural analyses and structural "action narratives" (as in A: "this acts as a tie, resisting the thrust of that truss," B: "no, those panels mean that the ties actually work to distribute wind load . . ." etc., etc.) are always possible; not because this engineer is right and that one wrong, but because the structure itself does not behave according to neatly computable categories. The possibility for creating "hybrid" structures (such as the Kimbell vault) that are traditionally un-analyzable because un-nameable is endless. Sufficiently detailed, so-called finite-element computer analysis and computer simulations could in principle make typological analyses obsolete, and with that make obsolete too the whole traditional language of "structures."

What has all this to do with Deconstruction? First, we might look at the name "deconstruction" again, and see metaphorized within it the twin processes of construction and demolition, processes that both bracket the life of the building-proper and point to its internal complexity, just as writing and criticism do to a text. But also one is put in mind of the notion of the infinite play of significations Derrida sees in language, the inherent undecidability of it all, and the way we must proceed nonetheless as though there were presences, elements, and canons. When an architect like Louis Kahn, and his engineer August Komendant, creates a new structure such as the cycloidal shell—one that in its visual simplicity strikes us as irreducible and yet works and "reads" undecidably—something truly marvelous has happened.

107. There is room for contention here. August Komendant is credited for proposing the cycloid shape as such. As a military engineer during World War II, he had reportedly used it in the design of tank and troop bridges. Even if we conceded that the cycloid offered some weight-strength-cost advantage, however, this advantage would surely be small relative to curves as close in shape as the ellipse. Komendant's bridges surely also did not have central, cross-ribbed skylight slots, which equally surely alter whatever fine structural felicity cycloids offered. No, what Kahn saw in Komendant's proposal was something in addition to and beyond structural efficiency, namely the metaphorical movement we now begin to discuss at some length, as well as "a pleasing aspect."

This, from Peter McCleary's essay in *Design Book Review* 11 (1987): 49.

Supporting the cycloid vault on columns rather than side walls . . . changes the structural behavior of the roof from vault to shell action, and it introduces the problem of the deformation of the long edge of the span. To control such deformations, Americans typically employ a stiff edge beam . . . whereas the European practitioner tends to place prestressing cables within the shell thickness. . . . In the Kimbell, a combination of means of resistance was used resulting in a hybrid roof structure that was neither pure vault nor pure shell. To further complicate matters, the elongation of the "vault-shell" caused it to behave as a beam curved in section.

While it is possible to understand and visualize a beam, *or* a vault, *or* a shell, McCleary explains, the level of abstraction required to visualize the structural operation of this hybrid and contradictory thing is considerable. A Deconstructionist is happy, and only a little surprised, to find this miscegenation of types, this elusiveness of reference, this dissemination of structural function. And we must disagree when McCleary continues that the difficulty we see here "obviates any . . . body-centered visual logic." On the contrary, to most of us the vaults look and feel intuitively just fine: athletic, remarkable, light, and correct, their tension internalized. Besides, whether or not something *is* a "vault," a "beam," a "plate," a whatever, is irrelevant, a matter of nomenclature, and a question of linguistic rather than structural systematics? As I have already noted, the fact is that most structures, *in operation,* operate hybridly, "self-deconstructively," always and already, their strength derived from what, it only seems to us, are different, clear, and originary structure-types in some kind of addition.

108. Of course, Kahn probably didn't want just "any old shape" here either. Early schemes show a number of vault profiles being considered, some quite square. The very esotericism of cycloids had its own value, a value in difficulty and originality for its own sake—or rather, for the sake of the questions it raises, such as "What's a cycloid, why a cycloid?" It is not difficult to believe that many of the geometrical sophistications of ancient Greek architecture—the slightly displaced and multiple radii at the amphitheater of Asclepias, for example—were done for the sheer joy of knowing how. Improvements in function or strength were largely imagined or simply put forward as pretext, so subtle or non-existent were they. The exercise of intellect in geometric esotericism was its own reward in a society whose world view held mathematics so high; and we, today, do not have to examine with undue earnestness the cosmic import, the gravity, the specific functional or religious significance of each and every geometrical inflection the Greeks came up with in their architecture.

109. I will omit resemblances to mannerist facades where a belt course may well adopt a similar formal rhythm, or to rows of arched dormer windows, and so on. I think these are superficial unless one wants to ask "why *do* A/B/A/B rhythms at all?" and this level of inquiry is precisely the one adopted by Derrida and myself here.

110. In classical arcades, the thickness/width of a column

serves adequately to separate the arches. Here, at the Kimbell, the crush between arches must be avoided too, but, because the columns are "inboard" of the arc, a separate device must be used to introduce the necessary spacing, namely, the interstitial seven-foot zones which when read classically, function as very wide columns.

Another explanation of the spacing between the vaults is tempting. One imagines a ball or cylinder rolling its full circumference once, and then contacting another cylinder, setting it to rolling its circumference once, contacting another, and so on. The diameter of a cylinder whose circumference is 23' 0" is 7' 4", or the rise of the vault, as well as the space between them. But because of the excess of 4", the system fails as an explanation. Kahn seemed not to be aware of, or chose to ignore, this potential relationship, basing his dimensioning instead on a centerline tartan grid, at the structural level, of 8' 0" for the service zone and 22'0" for the vault zone. (The 7' 0" and 23' 0" dimensions arise from a secondary adjustment having to do with material thicknesses.)

My thanks to colleague Larry Doll for proposing this explanation nonetheless. Had he known, I think Kahn might well have changed his dimensions scheme to make it true!

111. To the theme that architecture *is* (our best example of?) *arche-writing,* one might devote an entire book. I think that the outlines of this position are laid out within the text you now have in your hands, but a much closer reading of Derrida would be required to do justice to the notion.

On the theme that with the idea of *arche-writing* Derrida allows a positivistic foundationalism back into his system; see Jurgen Habermas, *Philosophical Discourse of Modernity.*

112. *Of Grammatology,* 69.

113. Ibid.

114. The issue opens up a whole discussion of modern urban and suburban planning practice. Developers find it easier to play a game of customizing repeated units than to shape the context in which the repetitions occur. The "crescenting" of suburban streets is a small move in the right direction, but only when the deeper idea that identifiable situation—position—with respect to the landscape and the other houses is the crucial variable is understood, will mat-

ters be significantly improved. Unfortunately, design at this public scale, care for landscape, and the willingness to engage difficult terrains—the three things required to change the background against which and within which the iterable individual gesture can be located—are more expensive, and the whole notion runs counter to the American ethos and economic system that privatizes and individualizes things in a common realm left wilderness.

115. Kahn himself may not have had much directly to do with the quality of design and layout here. Certainly, a tone had been set—a standard—by Kahn and Brown, and met by engineering consultants and workmen alike.

116. Look closely at the plan and you will see that everywhere solid walls pass through this servant zone, i.e. this seven-foot band, they are hollow: for electrical risers.

117. Doug Suisman, "The Design of the Kimbell: Variations on a Sublime Archetype," *Design Book Review* 11 (1987): 37.

118. Two, rather than one square because the lower level has a double-height room there. And of course one might say, in this formal dialectic, that this treatment of the conservator's court adds back, gives, a considerable amount of *wall* upon which to mount art.

119. The museum has had to use vertical louver blinds to control the light around this courtyard!

120. Earlier schemes for the Kimbell had many more vaults, and this west entry "court," it turns out, is indeed a *trace,* a halved remnant, of a full court in this position in a more extensive scheme.

121. We will never know, I suppose, whether Kahn himself seized and signed this moment, or whether the photographer urged him there.

122. Such is the creative nature of compiling and editing architectural texts, one might say.
    It is also the nature of what Derrida calls "the general text," this unauthored, continuous reverberation, iteration, displacement, and dissemination of figures through all ac-

tual meaning systems.

The Derridean interpretation, however, is not the only one, and even a deconstruction of the critical situation developing here would have to include the following, alternative narrative of explanation:

Many a scientific theory has been proved upon the occurrence of a small event. Einstein's General Theory of Relatively to this day, for example, though it "explains everything," is demonstrated directly only in infinitesimal "discrepancies" in the results of certain micro-physical and astrophysical measurements. The validity of countless other large systems of scientific explanation turn on the regular observation of similarly small and ephemeral phenomena.

On this parallel, the most fleeting of visual or functional events in the phenomenal sense can become invested with enormous importance in any system of ideas that predicts it. I think that this is the spirit in which Nell Johnson opposes text and photograph. John Lobell in *Between Silence and Light* does the same thing. Poems, and short excerpts from Kahn's long lectures, are grafted and lifted into a sort of prophetic status, prophecies which, like the best of those of physicists, can be caught instanced in a moment of realization. Kahn would have approved.

123. Report of Jane Brown, the wife of Richard Brown.

124. There is room for "old-fashioned" functional criticism here. Because the skylight could do no more than illuminate the vault, further lighting was required for the pictures. Where a courtyard does not provide rounded, natural light, recourse to incandescent "cans" is taken. The result is a mixture of light color which, I think, is regrettable. In places, the yellow light of these fixtures, with their steady, scalloped outlines, illuminates the art in a most pedestrian way, and Kahn's intention to make the light that falls on the art as natural and variable as the day, and therefore unique to the moment of viewing, is lost.

In addition, there are places where additional metal baffles, invisible to the visitor, are placed into the skylight: not only in the auditorium where the need was explicit (although Kahn *could* have chosen to eliminate the skylight entirely here) but adjacent to the north court where it was felt that there was light enough.

125. Kahn always tried to re-interpret the car as something more archaic, calling highways "viaducts," garages "silos," and so on.

Doug Suisman discusses this at greater length in his essay in *Design Book Review* 11.

126. From informal conversations with curators and "friends of the museum," and from books such as *In Pursuit of Quality*, it seems that this assertion would be quite strongly contested. If the argument goes that Kahn provided a variegated environment for curators to *work with* rather than a perfect museum with perfect lighting everywhere, and that this is a more enlightened attitude, then I concede. But we should not be oblivious to the costs of such an attitude, and I believe that one of them is the heaviness and physicality granted many large, or older, framed canvases when hung on flush, tooled walls, without moldings, etc., and with sometimes unfortunate lighting in glare and reflectivity (from the courtyards) as well as the shadows and color temperature of the incandescents relative to the cool wash from the vaults.

127. My referring to a non-existent street tries to bring to mind one of the contexts in which porticos in general make sense, function, and are even necessary, and which Kahn, in not having cars/carriages/horses/whatever alongside, was in a way mis-using. Interestingly, early plans of the area (provided by the City of Forth Worth) show a north-south street, poorly erased, (a genuine Derridean trace!) passing between the trees alongside the west entry on the way to the Exposition Center, representing a street that was never built but for which the trees were planted. This street was to have been named, I surmise, Will Rogers East, symmetric to Will Rogers West which exists on the west side of the site. Kahn could easily and quite usefully have resurrected Will Rogers East, but did not. (The whole Kimbell site was apparently to be a park/entry-grounds to the exposition center. Camp Bowie Boulevard ruined the plan for a U-shaped *allée* to the Center.)

In contrast, but along the same lines: Early pictures of the site show a rectangular grid/grove of trees in the southeast corner. These trees were evidently cut down for the Kimbell. Did Kahn consciously resurrect/iterate them for the west entry? I don't know. There is also a second grove of crape myrtles alongside the south entry, easily overlooked.

128. Louis Kahn, in *Light Is the Theme: Louis I. Kahn and the Kimbell Art Museum*, compiled by Nell E. Johnson (Fort Worth: Kimbell Art Foundation, 1975) 28.

129. Ibid.

130. A number of comparisons could begin to be made here between the Kimbell and the de Menil Museum in Houston by Renzo Piano. Piano was obviously inspired by the Kimbell. A low and calm building with a fetishized overhead lighting system, the true similarities stop about there. The matter of entry that we are discussing here (the de Menil's "vaults" are continuous around) is just one example where the Kimbell beats the Menil.

131. In his *Philosophy of Fine Art*, vol. 3, Hegel describes architecture as the most fundamental of the arts, itself divided into three stages of evolution. The first of these, dubbed the "symbolic," occurs when man, holding back chaos, nature, and the elements, first makes a place of habitation for himself and for his god(s)—the hut and the temple respectively—and enlarges them for gathering.

Architecture is in fact the first pioneer on the highway towards the adequate realization of the Godhead. In this service it is put to severe labour with objective nature, that it may disengage it(self) by its effort from the confused growth of finitude and the distortions of contingency. By this means it levels a space for the God, informs His external environment, and builds Him His temple, as a fit place for the concentration of Spirit, and its direction to the absolute objects of everyday life. (chap. 5, trans. Osmaston, 1920; reprinted in Dickie and Sclafani, *Aesthetics* [New York: St Martin's, 1977] 533.)

   "Hegel imagined the men who built the first temples as they cleared the ground on which to build them [describing], this as 'clearing the undergrowth of finitude'," says H. B. Acton in the *Encyclopaedia of Philosophy,* obviously using a different translation for his quotation.   Of course, it is Heidegger who picks up the themes of clearing, inhabiting, gathering etc. . . . metaphorizing them to apply to/describe

Dasein itself, placing thus the ideas of "absencing" and "readiness" before "presencing," and so on. Said Heidegger: "a realm of being . . . opens up when the earth becomes a habitation. The home and dwelling of mortals has its own natural site . . . but . . . marked out and opened by something of another order." (*What Is Called Thinking*, 191).

In his well-known essay "Building, Dwelling, Thinking" we see Hegel's "history of architecture" developed by Heidegger into a larger field of reference, only ambiguously, I believe, about architecture itself.

132. The grove also literally re-creates, displaces, and replaces a similar gridded grove that existed on the southeastern corner of the site before the Kimbell was erected, as I noted earlier (note 127). Does the grove *recall* the first one? More accurately, does it make *us* recall the first one? One has to know of the first one first, perhaps through true texts such as this, and then forget it in some sense, and then remember it again in the experience of the one that is there now. This rather crude and lengthy mechanism is typically invoked in mnemonic theories of architectural meaning (based on the ancient Roman "method of loci") that would describe how architectural meaning works in general. Language-like, because it attaches signs to signifiers so clearly, a mnemonic theory in fact describes only a very small set of architecture's means and meanings, as I hope this essay is proving.

133. I am grateful to Kenneth Frampton for pointing out this reading (personal communication).

134. In part as a result of this orientation, until recent times there has not been a strong tradition of Jewish painting, sculpture, or architecture, neither in terms of any "Jewishness" as such, nor in the achievement of some consistent, notable, quality-in-general by Jewish individuals. Historical reasons for this are many and cannot be gone into here.

135. I should also mention that, as a Jew, this was my own ideological home environment.

For an excellent essay on Kahn's Jewish heritage, and the influence on him of Kabbalism and German Idealist philosophy, see Joseph Burton, "Notes from Volume Zero: Louis Kahn and the Language of God," *Perspecta* 20 (1983): 69-90.

For material touching on Jewishness in relation to recent architecture, see Stanley Tigerman's books *Versus: An American Architect's Alternatives* (New York: Rizzoli, 1982) and *The Architecture of Exile.*

Cf. also Charles Jencks's interview with Peter Eisenman in *Deconstruction in Architecture, Architectural Design Profile.*

136. We note that Derrida might not want to go along with the hierarchy implied here by "prior" and "closer to"; this although *his* use of the prefix *"arche"* seems to induce this very cognitive structure, as Habermas *(Philosophical Discourse of Modernity)* also notes.

137. I say for the first time because Kahn's first museum commission at Yale University was for modern art, which is mostly abstract.

138. From R. S. Wurman, ed., *What Will Be Has Always Been: The Words of Louis I. Kahn* (New York: Rizzoli, 1986) 218.

139. Ibid., 250, 223.

140. In Kahn, *Light is the Theme*, 11.

141. A point well made by Joseph Burton, op. cit.

142. For a beginning in this enterprise, see Mark Angelil, "Construction Deconstructed: A Relative Reading of Architectural Technology," *Journal of Architectural Education* 40 (Spring 1987): 24-31. For a somewhat deconstructive view of Mies Van der Rohe, see Caroline Constant, "The Barcelona Pavilion."

Of course, there is no reason why a new and Deconstructionist project of the analysis of (preferably still-standing) seminal works of architecture down through history could not be embarked upon. Oppositions between the Romanticism and Rationalism of various periods, for example, invite deconstructive analysis of the specific works put forward to exemplify each. This would undoubtedly show the infection with, and suppression of, one in the other in the building itself. Moreover, a double-deconstruction of sorts would certainly be possible, and likely be quite productive, when any accompanying texts or ideologies are brought into play.

143. J. Hillis Miller, cited in Culler, *On Deconstruction,* 269.

144. Ibid.

145. Jacques Derrida, in "Fragments of a Conversation with Jacques Derrida," *Precis* 66 (1987): 49.

Other Titles from Lumen, Inc.

Dialogue in the Void:
Beckett & Giacometti
Matti Megged
ISBN: 0-930829-01-8

Culture and Politics in Nicaragua:
Testimonies of Poets and Writers
Steven White
ISBN: 0-930829-02-6

Sor Juana's Dream
Edited and translated by Luis Harss
ISBN: 0-930829-07-7

For an Architecture of Reality
Michael Benedikt
ISBN: 0-930829-05-0

Reverse Thunder,
A Dramatic Poem
Diane Ackerman
ISBN: 0-930829-09-3

Space in Motion
Juan Goytisolo
Translated by Helen Lane
ISBN: 0-930829-03-4

Borges in/and/on Film
Edgardo Cozarinsky
Translated by Gloria Waldman and
Ronald Christ
ISBN: 0-930829-08-5

Written on a Body
Severo Sarduy
Translated by Carol Maier
ISBN: 0-930829-04-2

ANGST: Cartography
Moji Baratloo & Cliff Balch
ISBN: 0-930829-10-7

SITES
An annual literary/architectural magazine
ISSN: 0747-9409